Best Easy Day Hikes Series

Best Easy Day Hikes
Reno

SO-BCO-459

Tracy Salcedo-Chourré

FALCONGUIDES

GUILFORD, CONNECTICUT
HELENA, MONTANA

AN IMPRINT OF GLOBE PEQUOT PRESS

FALCONGUIDES®

Copyright © 2010 by Morris Book Publishing, LLC

FalconGuides is an imprint of Globe Pequot Press.

Falcon, FalconGuides, and Outfit Your Mind are registered trademarks
of Morris Book Publishing, LLC.

TOPO! Explorer software and SuperQuad source maps courtesy of
National Geographic Maps. For information about TOPO! Explorer,
TOPO!, and Nat Geo Maps products, go to www.topo.com or www
.natgeomaps.com.

Maps: Offroute Inc. © Morris Book Publishing, LLC

Project editor: David Legere
Layout: Kevin Mak

Library of Congress Cataloging-in-Publication Data
Salcedo-Chourré, Tracy.
  Best easy day hikes, Reno / Tracey Salcedo-Chourré.
    p. cm. — (Faclonguides)
  ISBN 978-0-7627-5110-5
  1. Hiking—Nevada—Reno—Guidebooks. 2. Trails—Nevada—
Reno—Guidebooks. 3. Nevada—Guidebooks. I.Title.
  GV199.42.N3S35 2010
  917.93'550434–dc22
                                        2010005597
Printed in the United States of America

10 9 8 7 6 5 4 3 2 1

Contents

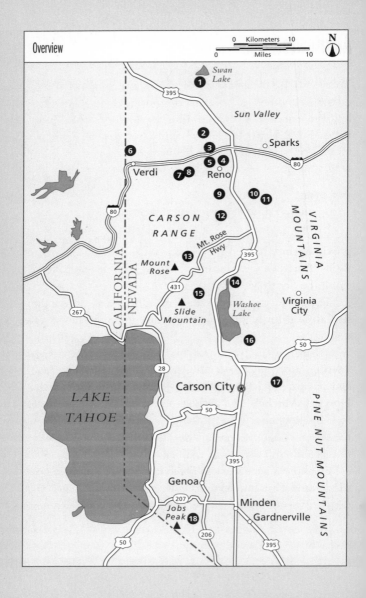

0   Kilometers   10

0   Miles   10

N

Swan Lake
1

Sun Valley

395

2

3

Sparks

6

5   4

80

Verdi   7 8   Reno

9

10 11

CARSON
RANGE

12

VIRGINIA
MOUNTAINS

80

Mt. Rose Hwy

395

13

Mount
Rose

431

14

15

Washoe
Lake

Virginia
City

Slide
Mountain

16

50

28

17

Carson City

PINE NUT MOUNTAINS

LAKE
TAHOE

50

CALIFORNIA
NEVADA

267

395

Genoa

207

Minden

Jobs
Peak   18

Gardnerville

50

206

395

Acknowledgments

Thanks to the local trail experts who took time to answer questions and review hike descriptions, including Billy Sibley, open space and trails coordinator for the City of Reno Parks, Recreation, and Community Services Department; Cheryl Surface, park planner with the Washoe County Department of Regional Parks & Open Space; Arthur Callen of the Bureau of Land Management's Carson City District; and Donna Silver at Washoe Lake State Park. Thanks also to Steve Hale, trails coordinator for the Humboldt-Toiyabe National Forest, Carson City Ranger District, for providing information about trail access and maintenance issues. An extra shout-out to Billy Sibley for escorting me along the South Meadows Trail.

Thanks to the expert team of editors and production staff at GPP for helping me make this guide the best it can be.

Thanks to family and friends who support my work as a writer, especially Sarah Chourré, Nick and Chris Salcedo, and my parents Jesse and Judy. The Friedman clan—Rita, Howard, Mitchell, and Debby—are family, too, and I am forever grateful for being able to make their lovely home on the shores of Lake Tahoe my base of operations. Thanks also to Ian, Grace, Tory, Zoe, and Cami.

Finally, my gratitude always to my husband, Martin, and sons, Jesse, Cruz, and Penn, who never complain when I take off for the hills without them—or when I drag them along.

About the Author

Tracy Salcedo-Chourré has written more than a score of guidebooks to destinations in California and Colorado, including *Hiking Lassen Volcanic National Park, Exploring California's Missions and Presidios, Exploring Point Reyes National Seashore and the Golden Gate National Recreation Area, Best Rail-Trails California,* and *Best Easy Day Hikes* guides to the San Francisco Bay Area, Lake Tahoe, Reno, Sacramento, Boulder, Denver, and Aspen.

She is also an editor, teacher, and soccer mom—but somehow still finds time to hike, cycle, swim, and garden. She lives with her husband, three sons, and a small menagerie of pets in California's Wine Country.

You can learn more by visiting her Web page at the FalconGuide site, www.falcon.com/user/172. Her guidebooks are available online through Falcon/GPP, at various outdoor shops, and through local and national booksellers.

Introduction

I'll admit it at the outset: Reno-area trails were mostly a mystery to me before I started researching this book. Years of hiking in the mountains on the Nevada side of Lake Tahoe offered tantalizing glimpses into the Truckee Meadows, Washoe Valley, and Carson River valley below, but not enough to lure me out of the magnetic Sierra Nevada.

But it turns out Reno's parks and open spaces are magnetic too. Step outside the doors of the casino—or the door of your home in the downtown area, the North Valleys, or the South Valley—and you'll find an evolving network of pathways that ventures into the striking hills, ranges, and riparian zones that define the westernmost reaches of the Great Basin.

The transition zone between the lower montane habitat of the Sierra and the high desert of the Great Basin is dynamic, and several trails in the guide skim in and out of this ecotone. On the high side the paths reach into yellow pine forests with a distinctly mountainous feel; on the low side they drop into a scrubland dominated by sagebrush, bitterbrush, and desert peach. After a thunderstorm or when in bloom, the desert plants perfume the air with a heady, savory-sweet fragrance.

The Truckee River also informs Reno's hiking landscape. Clear and swift, the Truckee runs right through the middle of town on its 110-mile descent from Lake Tahoe to Pyramid Lake. Trail planners have made good use of this asset, building popular routes that follow the riverbed and snake along its tributaries. The river and surrounding streams, including Galena, Whites, and Thomas Creeks, support complex riparian habitats and saturate wetlands that support a wealth of bird, plant, and animal life.

The area's history also underlays its trail system. Ditches—the Steamboat, Last Chance, and Highland to name a few—and flumes were used to transport lumber from the high country and power the mills of Nevada's mining industry, including the famed Comstock Lode in the Virginia Range at historic Virginia City. When the silver ore of the Comstock played out, the ditches were used to irrigate the rangeland and support ranching and agriculture in the high desert valleys. These days, easy trails run alongside portions of the historic ditches, popular with hikers, cyclists, and trail runners alike.

Each hike in this guide is unique for its ecology, history, topography, or natural beauty. My intent is for these routes to serve as gateways; if the trail described here doesn't fit your needs, you can be sure another in that park or a neighboring open space will.

From the banks of the glittering Truckee to the dry summits of the Huffaker Hills, from the Hole in the Wall to Deadman's Overlook, I hope you find these treks as satisfying as I have.

The Nature of Reno

Reno's trails range from the rugged and hilly to the flat and paved. Hikes in this guide cover the gamut. While by definition a best easy day hike is not strenuous and poses little danger to the traveler, knowing a few details about the nature of the Reno area will enhance your explorations.

Weather
Reno lies in the high desert at about 4,400 feet in elevation, with low humidity and lots of sunshine. The best weather

for hiking is in spring and fall, when high temperatures range from the 40s to the 70s, but the weather, with a few caveats, is conducive to hiking year-round.

An average of 7.5 inches of rain falls in the area annually, mostly in winter and during springtime thunderstorms. Snowfall averages 25 inches annually, mostly in small doses of 1 to 2 inches at a time, and generally melts off quickly. Winter lows plunge into the 20s and 30s, while highs creep into the low 40s. When hiking in winter, carry layers of clothing to insulate yourself from the cold and potential rain or snow.

Summertime temperatures are not oppressive for a desert, with averages in the 80s and 90s. The occasional heat wave can drive temps into the 100s. Temperature variations can be extreme, however, with nighttime lows dropping into the 40s and 50s. Hiking in the morning or evening is recommended, since the combination of heat and low humidity can lead to rapid dehydration. No matter the trail's length or the amount of shade along the route, carry plenty of water. Morning and evening hours not only mitigate the risks of heat-related illness, they offer lovely light and a greater opportunity to see wildlife.

Critters

You'll encounter mostly benign creatures on these trails, such as squirrels, rabbits, lizards, and a variety of birdlife. More rarely seen are coyotes, deer, and raccoons. Encounters with wildlife that pose a potential threat to hikers are even more rare but are definitely possible, so beware the black bear, mountain lion, and venomous snake.

Nevada is home to five species of pit vipers, including the western diamondback and Great Basin rattlesnakes.

Snakes generally only strike if they are threatened—you are too big to be dinner, so they typically avoid contact with humans. Keep your distance, and they will keep theirs. If you encounter a snake on the trail, back away slowly. Use caution when climbing over rocks or venturing into caves. Snakes are also known to seek shelter under cars in hot weather.

Mountain lions are most active at dawn and dusk. Like snakes they generally avoid contact with humans, but to further reduce the chances of an encounter, make noise while hiking. Don't jog or ride a bike in areas where a lion has been sighted, as those activities mimic prey behavior. If you come across a mountain lion, make yourself as big as possible and do not run. If you don't act like or look like prey, you stand a good chance of not being attacked. If the attack comes anyway, fight back.

Black bear encounters usually involve some kind of food, whether left in a car, a tent, a garbage can, or on a windowsill. They've been known to remove windshields from automobiles to get at coolers and to stroll through the open doors of homes to rummage in refrigerators. If you encounter a bear on the trail, do not run. Stand still, make noise, and the bear will generally scram. Never come between a mama bear and her cubs; if you see cubs, leave the area immediately.

Be Prepared

Hikers should be prepared for any situation, whether they are out for a short stroll along the Truckee River in downtown Reno or venturing into secluded Fay Canyon. Some specific advice:

- Know the basics of first aid, including how to treat bleeding, bites and stings, and fractures, strains, and sprains. Pack a first-aid kit on each excursion.

- Familiarize yourself with the symptoms of heat exhaustion and heatstroke. Heat exhaustion symptoms include heavy sweating, muscle cramps, headache, dizziness, and fainting. Should you or any of your hiking party exhibit any of these symptoms, cool the victim down immediately by rehydrating and getting him or her to an air-conditioned location. Cold showers also help reduce body temperature. Heatstroke is much more serious. The victim may lose consciousness and the skin is hot and dry to the touch. Call 911 immediately.

- Regardless of the weather, your body needs a lot of water while hiking. Consuming a full 32-ounce bottle is the minimum for these short hikes, but more is always better.

- Don't drink from streams, rivers, creeks, or lakes without treating or filtering the water first. Waterways and water bodies may host a variety of contaminants, including giardia, which can cause serious intestinal unrest.

- Prepare for extremes of both heat and cold by dressing in layers.

- Carry a backpack in which you can store extra clothing, ample drinking water and food, and whatever goodies, like guidebooks, cameras, and binoculars, you might want.

- Some area trails have cell phone coverage. Bring your device, but make sure you've turned it off or got it on the vibrate setting while hiking. Nothing like a wake-the-dead–loud ring to startle every creature in the area, including fellow hikers. On longer hikes, turning off your phone also conserves the battery charge for use in case of emergency.

- Keep children under careful watch. Have them carry a plastic whistle; if they become lost, they should stay in one place and blow the whistle to summon help.

Zero Impact

Trails in the Reno area are heavily used year-round. We, as trail users and advocates, must be especially vigilant to make sure our passage leaves no lasting mark. Here are some basic guidelines for preserving trails in the region:

- Pack out all your own trash, including biodegradable items like orange peels. You might also pack out garbage left by less-considerate hikers.

- Avoid damaging trailside soils and plants by remaining on the established route. Social trails created by hikers, cyclists, and off-road vehicles are a plague on area parklands, contributing to erosion problems and creating unsightly scars on the landscape. Don't cut switchbacks, which can promote erosion.

- Don't approach or feed any wild creatures—the squirrel eyeing your snack food is best able to survive if it remains self-reliant.

- Don't pick wildflowers or gather rocks, antlers, feathers, and other treasures along the trail. Removing these items will only take away from the next hiker's experience.

- Be courteous by not making loud noises while hiking.

- Many of these trails are multiuse, which means you'll share them with other hikers, trail runners, mountain bikers, and equestrians. Familiarize yourself with the proper trail etiquette, yielding the trail when appropriate.

- Use outhouses at trailheads or along the trail.

Reno Area Boundaries and Corridors

All hikes are within a one-hour drive from downtown Reno. Most hikes are in the Truckee Meadows and adjacent North and South Valleys, but some reach westward into the Sierra foothills and south into the Washoe and Carson River valleys.

Two major highways intersect in Reno—I-80, which runs east-west, and US 395, which runs north-south. Trailhead directions are given from these highways. McCarran Boulevard circles the metropolitan area, offering easy alternative access to trails.

Land Management

The following government agencies manage most of the public lands described in this guide and can provide further information on these hikes and other trails in their service areas.

- City of Reno's Parks, Recreation and Community Services Department, 190 East Liberty St. (P.O. Box 1900), Reno 89505; (775) 334-2262; www.cityofreno.com

- Washoe County Department of Regional Parks and Open Space, 2601 Plumas St., Reno 89509; (775) 823-6500; www.washoecountyparks.com. A downloadable guide to the county parks is available on the Web site.

- Nevada Division of State Parks, Washoe Lake State Park, 4855 East Lake Blvd., Carson City 89704; (775) 687-4319; http://parks.nv.gov/wl.htm

- Bureau of Land Management, Carson City District, 5665 Morgan Mill Rd., Carson City 89701; (775) 885-6000; www.blm.gov
- Humboldt-Toiyabe National Forest, Carson Ranger District, 1536 South Carson St., Carson City 89701; (775) 882-2766; www.fs.fed.us/r4/htnf

Nevada Trail Maps.com, an online trails clearinghouse created and maintained by the University of Nevada, Reno's Great Basin Institute, provides information and detailed maps for routes throughout the state. Visit www.nvtrail maps.com to research trails and download maps. Contact information is Great Basin Institute, University of Nevada, Reno, Mailstop 0099, Reno 89557; (775) 784-1192.

A couple of area hiking associations also provide online information about local trails.

- The Truckee Meadows Trails Association maintains trail descriptions of area routes on its Web site, www .truckeemeadowstrails.org.
- The Carson Valley Trails Association Web site includes information about trails in the Carson River valley. Visit www.carsonvalleytrails.org.

Public Transportation

Public transportation for Reno is provided by the Regional Transportation Commission (RTC), which operates a number of bus routes in the city and to outlying communities, including Carson City. Route information is available at www.rtcwashoe.com. Call (775) 348-RIDE for more information.

How to Use This Guide

This guide is designed to be simple and easy to use. Each hike is described with a map and summary information that delivers the trail's vital statistics including length, difficulty, fees and permits, park hours, canine compatibility, and trail contacts. Directions to the trailhead are also provided, along with a general description of what you'll see along the way. A detailed route finder (Miles and Directions) sets forth mileages between significant landmarks along the trail.

How the Hikes Were Chosen

This guide describes trails that are accessible to every hiker, whether visiting from out of town or a local resident. The hikes are no longer than 6 miles round-trip, and most are considerably shorter, with an emphasis on interpretive nature trails. They range in difficulty from flat excursions perfect for a family outing to more challenging treks in the foothills of the Sierra. While these trails are among the best, keep in mind that nearby trails, sometimes in the same park or sometimes in a neighboring open space, may offer options better suited to your needs. Where applicable, alternatives are suggested in the Options section at the end of hike descriptions. I've selected hikes in the North Valleys area, Truckee Meadows proper, and in the Washoe and Carson River valleys, so wherever your starting point you'll find a great easy day hike nearby.

Selecting a Hike

These are all easy hikes, but easy is a relative term. Some would argue that no hike involving any kind of climbing is easy, but climbs are a fact of life in the Reno area.

- **Easy** hikes are generally short and flat, taking no longer than an hour to complete.
- **Moderate** hikes involve increased distance and relatively mild changes in elevation, and will take one to two hours to complete.
- **More challenging** hikes feature some steep stretches, greater distances, and generally take longer than two hours to complete.

Keep in mind that what you think is easy is entirely dependent on your level of fitness and the adequacy of your gear (primarily shoes). Use the trail's length as a gauge of its relative difficulty—even if climbing is involved it won't be bad if the hike is less than 1 mile long. The Trail Finder lists Best Long Hikes, which are more strenuous than others due to length and elevation changes. If you are hiking with a group, select a hike that's appropriate for the least fit and prepared in your party.

Approximate hiking times are based on the assumption that on flat ground, most walkers average 2 miles per hour. Adjust that rate by the steepness of the terrain and your level of fitness (subtract time if you're an aerobic animal and add time if you're hiking with kids), and you have a ballpark hiking duration. Be sure to add more time if you plan to picnic or take part in other activities like bird watching or photography.

Trail Finder

Best Hikes for River Lovers

Best Hikes for Great Views

Best Hikes for Nature Lovers

Best Hikes for Children

Best Hikes for Dogs

Best Hikes for Birders

Best Long Hikes

Map Legend

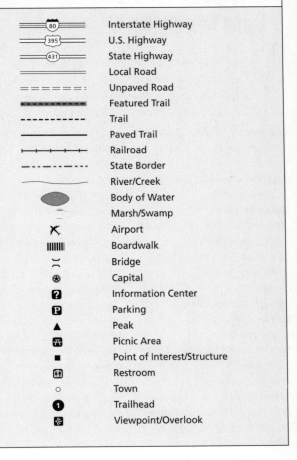

80	Interstate Highway
395	U.S. Highway
431	State Highway
	Local Road
	Unpaved Road
	Featured Trail
	Trail
	Paved Trail
	Railroad
	State Border
	River/Creek
	Body of Water
	Marsh/Swamp
✗	Airport
▥	Boardwalk
⌣	Bridge
⊛	Capital
❷	Information Center
ℙ	Parking
▲	Peak
⛻	Picnic Area
■	Point of Interest/Structure
⌁	Restroom
○	Town
❶	Trailhead
⚘	Viewpoint/Overlook

1 South Side Interpretive Trail and Boardwalk

A trail and a boardwalk lead into the Swan Lake Nature Study Area and onto Swan Lake itself, where birds and hikers alike find a watery refuge in the desert.

Distance: 1.4 miles out and back on trail; 0.5 mile out and back on boardwalk

Approximate hiking time: 1.5 hours

Difficulty: Easy

Trail surface: Dirt and gravel singletrack; boardwalk

Best seasons: Spring and fall; avoid the unshaded trails on hot summer days

Other trail users: None

Canine compatibility: Leashed dogs permitted

Land status: Swan Lake Nature Study Area

Fees and permits: None

Schedule: Park hours are from 8:00 a.m. to 9:00 p.m. June to Sept; 8:00 a.m. to 7:00 p.m. Sept to Nov; 8:00 a.m. to 5:00 p.m. Nov to Mar; and 8:00 a.m. to 7:00 p.m. Mar to June

Trailhead amenities: Restrooms, a covered picnic shelter, and trash receptacles

Maps: USGS Reno NE; www.nvtrailmaps.com

Trail contacts: Washoe County Department of Regional Parks and Open Space, 2601 Plumas St., Reno 89509; (775) 823-6500; www.washoecountyparks.com. Lahontan Audubon Society, P.O. Box 2304, Reno, 89505; (775) 324-BIRD (2473); www.nevadaaudubon.org.

Other: Bring binoculars and a guidebook to help you identify the birds that live near or visit the lake. The boardwalk section of the trail is handicapped accessible.

Finding the trailhead: From the intersection of I-80 and US 395 in downtown Reno, head north on US 395 for 8 miles to the Lemmon Drive exit. Go right (east) on Lemmon Drive for 1 mile to Military Road and turn left (north). Follow Military Road for 1.6 miles to Lear Boulevard. Turn right (east) on Lear Boulevard and go 0.4 mile to the end of the pavement. Head left (north) for 0.2 mile on the dirt road signed for the Swan Lake Nature Study Area to the trailhead and parking area. GPS: N39 39.024' / W119 51.395'

The Hike

The two prongs of this tour of the Swan Lake Nature Study Area venture into vastly different environments, though that won't be evident from the trailhead. Especially in dry years you'll see nothing but high desert scrubland stretching to the north and west, with no hint that Swan Lake exists at all.

The natural area has a rather unnatural setting, bordered by warehouses on the south and west and by wastewater treatment ponds on the east. The shallow lake and its surrounding wetlands, fed by meltwater from Peavine Peak to the southwest and treated wastewater (so no swimming or fishing), can be as small as 100 acres or as large as 1,000 acres, depending on the amount of rainfall and runoff. Conditions will dictate whether the lake will be visible from the trailhead or trail, but generally the boardwalk ends up on the water. The boardwalk is so easy it can be walked in flip-flops and is perfect for the elderly, infirm, and children. Constructed of recycled plastic boards, the floating walkway winds through a cattail–filled marsh to a viewing deck overlooking an expanse of dark water where ducks, geese, coots, swans, stilts, and avocets may be spotted.

The flat, easy South Side Interpretive Trail leads into a typical northern Nevada scrubland, with views of rolling brown hills to the north and east and Peavine Peak rising above the industrial complex to the southwest. Carpeted in bitterbrush, sages, and desert peach, the brush is habitat for a variety of songbirds—swallows, blackbirds, and wrens—as well as raptors such as burrowing owls, northern harriers, and gold and bald eagles. Walk softly and quail are likely to scurry across the path in front of you, sparrows watch from the tops of bushes, and garter snakes slither from trail's edge to the safety of nearby rocks.

Begin by following the raised gravel path to an information signboard ringed by benches, where the boardwalk and interpretive trail separate. You can do either or both: The interpretive trail is described first, then the boardwalk.

The interpretive trail leads first to a molded plastic blind in the form of a low rock wall. The mock-rock structure is posted with interpretive plaques and offers birders a chance to identify avian species without disturbing them.

From the blind the singletrack climbs almost imperceptibly into the scrub, with some sections white and alkaline, others sandy, and others paved in gravel. Turn around when you reach the dirt roadway that stretches north and south along the western boundary of the natural area, then return to the trail junction to meet the boardwalk.

A gravel path approaches a clump of cottonwood and willow, where you'll cross a bridge onto the recycled plastic boardwalk. Interpretive signs describe everything from how wastewater is used to maintain the marsh to the species of birds, mammals, and amphibians you're likely to see as you explore. Benches and viewing platforms allow space to rest and observe. The boardwalk ends on open water where, depending on the season, a variety of ducks, coots, and other shorebirds play, feed, snort, and rumble on the water.

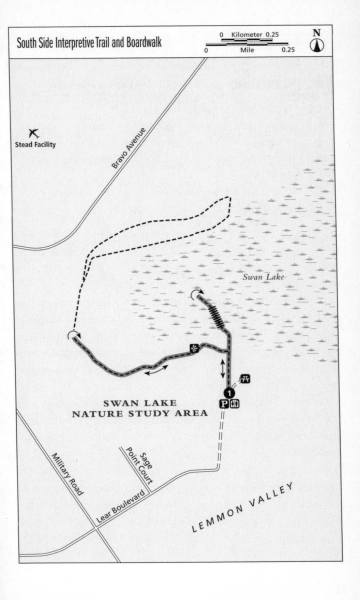

South Side Interpretive Trail and Boardwalk

0   Kilometer   0.25

0   Mile   0.25

N

Stead Facility

Bravo Avenue

Swan Lake

SWAN LAKE
NATURE STUDY AREA

1

Military Road

Sage Point Court

Lear Boulevard

LEMMON VALLEY

Enjoy the sights and sounds, then return as you came to the trailhead.

Miles and Directions

0.0   Start by heading north on the gravel path.

0.1   The trail splits at the information signboard. Go left (west) on the singletrack South Side Interpretive Trail.

0.2   Arrive at the mock-rock blind. Continue west on the obvious singletrack.

0.7   Arrive at the dirt roadway; this is the turnaround point.

1.3   Arrive back at the trail junction at the information signboard. Turn left (north) to reach the boardwalk.

1.5   Arrive at the observation deck at the end of the boardwalk overlooking the lake.

1.9   Arrive back at the trailhead and parking area.

2 Evans Canyon and Miner's Trail Loop

Trace the course of little Evans Creek through a steep–sided canyon, venturing into a high desert landscape that feels secluded despite being embedded in suburban Reno.

Distance: 3.5-mile lollipop loop
Approximate hiking time: 2 to 3 hours
Difficulty: More challenging due to trail length and surface
Trail surface: Dirt singletrack
Best seasons: Winter, spring, late fall. Avoid the shadeless trail in the heat of summer.
Other trail users: Mountain bikers, trail runners
Canine compatibility: Leashed dogs permitted
Land status: Rancho San Rafael Regional Park
Fees and permits: None
Schedule: Park hours are from 8:00 a.m. to 9:00 p.m. June to Sept; 8:00 a.m. to 7:00 p.m. Sept to Nov; 8:00 a.m. to 5:00 p.m. Nov to Mar; and 8:00 a.m. to 7:00 p.m. Mar to June
Trailhead amenities: There is ample parking at the trailhead, along with a restroom and trash cans.
Maps: USGS Reno; www.nvtrail maps.com
Trail contacts: Washoe County Department of Regional Parks and Open Space, 2601 Plumas St., Reno 89509; (775) 823-6500; www.washoecountyparks.com.
Special considerations: Do not venture onto this exposed trail without ample drinking water. Do not drink from the stream. Rattlesnakes are sometimes seen along the trail.

Finding the trailhead: From I-80 take the downtown Reno/Virginia Street exit. Go north on North Virginia Street for 1.2 miles, past the University of Nevada, Reno (UNR) campus and the junction with North McCarran Boulevard, to the left-hand (west) turnoff into the well-signed Reno Sports Complex. The trailhead is at the west end of the parking lot. GPS: N39 33.213' / W119 49.779'

The Hike

You can't miss the first stop on this route—the massive abstract Basque monument, commemorating the contributions of Basque sheepherders. Striking as the big blue sculpture is, little Evans Creek proves the more fascinating feature on the landscape, winding through a steep-walled desert canyon and watering small riparian gardens.

One of several streams that spill down and around Peavine Peak, Evans Creek winds through high desert scrub that flowers beautifully in spring, with delicate pink blooms on the desert peach and pastel yellow flowers on the bitterbrush. Though the flow is relatively placid even in the runoff season, the creek has carved itself a relatively secluded canyon, a rare escape close in to downtown Reno.

The trail begins and ends on an interpretive nature trail in the shadow of the monument (and on the edge of a disk golf course). Visit the monument first, then descend to the nature trail along the banks of the creek. Interpretive signs line this stretch of the route. Side trails carved by mountain bikers and other hikers wing out in different directions, but the main trail is well trod and obvious.

Leaving the nature trail behind, the Evans Canyon Trail heads down into a steep-walled canyon, with neighborhood homes perched on the lip above to the right (east). To the west, steep slopes climb up onto Peavine Peak, undeveloped save for power poles, the slashes of dirt roads, and the painted N sign of school spirit for nearby UNR. On cool mornings and evenings, students in running shoes and on mountain bikes take to the trail in small swarms, so be prepared to share.

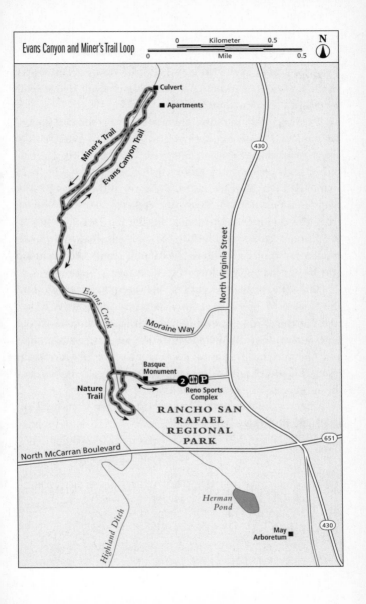

Evans Canyon and Miner's Trail Loop

N

0   Kilometer   0.5

0   Mile   0.5

Culvert
Apartments

Miner's Trail

Evans Canyon Trail

Evans Creek

430

North Virginia Street

Moraine Way

Basque Monument

2

Reno Sports Complex

Nature Trail

RANCHO SAN RAFAEL REGIONAL PARK

North McCarran Boulevard

651

Highland Ditch

Herman Pond

May Arboretum

430

Pass several trail junctions and cross to the east side of the creek as you continue upstream. By the time you reach the first junction with the Miner's Trail (the return route) you'll have lost sight of most signs of civilization, though they'll soon make encore appearances.

Farther along, the canyon widens, giving the creek space to pool and watering springtime gardens of pentstemon, aster, geranium, wild rose, and sage. The trail is occasionally paved with broken rock from small slides. Beyond the mile mark the creek spreads into a meadow and tailings piles—plant-free mounds of yellow- and red-streaked earth—hang from the opposite canyon wall. At the head of the canyon, the route skirts the foundations of apartment buildings, crosses in front of a culvert, then meets the Miner's Trail and begins its descent down the west side of the canyon.

The downstream stretch is highlighted by views into the Carson Range. Hitch up with the Evans Canyon Trail again at the 2-mile mark, then with the nature trail. Lined with interpretive signs describing the area's geology, flora, and fauna, the nature trail closes the loop, circling a pond choked with cattails. Finish by climbing past the Basque monument to the trailhead.

Miles and Directions

0.0   Start by passing through the gate and following the broad path toward the towering blue Basque monument.

0.1   Arrive at the monument. Check out the plaques, then circle around and head down the broad track, crossing over the Highland Ditch via a plank bridge as you descend.

0.3   Reach the junction with the nature trail at an interpretive sign in the creek drainage. Stay straight (right/northwest) on the main track. In less than 0.1 mile, cross the shallow stream and reach a second nature trail junction at a bench. Stay right (north) on the Evans Canyon Trail; the nature trail bends left (west). Climb into an open area filled with braided trails; the EVANS CANYON TRAILHEAD sign is obvious to the right (northeast).

0.6 At the intersection with an unsigned trail, stay right (north).

0.7 Reach the junction with the signed Updike Ravine Trail. Stay right (north) on the Evans Canyon Trail, with the stream now on the left (west) side.

1.0 Arrive at the intersection with the Miner's Trail. Stay right (north) on the Evans Canyon Trail.

1.5 Climb past the foundations of apartment buildings to the head of the canyon at a staircase and culvert. Pass in front of the culvert and pick up the Miner's Trail on the west face of the canyon atop a tailings pile.

1.8 Cross a second tailings pile.

2.1 Arrive back at the junction with the Evans Canyon Trail. Cross the creek onto the Evans Canyon route and retrace your steps to the junction with the nature trail. (You can also stay on the Miner's Trail and rejoin the Evans Canyon Trail farther downstream.)

2.8 At the junction with the interpretive trail, go right (south-west), following the thoroughly signed route around the over-grown pond and through the rich riparian zone.

3.3 Arrive at the junction with the trail that climbs back east toward the Basque monument.

3.5 Arrive back at the trailhead.

3 May Arboretum and Herman Pond

Just minutes from downtown Reno, the May Arboretum and surrounding parklands provide a fine short hike with great views and an easy-to-enjoy botany lesson.

Distance: 1.1-mile loop
Approximate hiking time: 1 hour
Difficulty: Easy
Trail surface: Pavement; decomposed granite pathways
Best seasons: Spring and fall for blooms and autumn color, but the arboretum can be enjoyed year-round if you avoid extremes of summer heat and winter cold
Other trail users: None in the arboretum; mountain bikers near Herman Pond
Canine compatibility: No dogs permitted in the arboretum, but it's a dog off-leash paradise in the huge fenced pasture to the west. Dogs must be leashed in other areas of the park.
Land status: Rancho San Rafael Regional Park
Fees and permits: None for the arboretum, but a fee is charged if you want to tour the May Museum or play in the Great Basin Adventure area.

Schedule: Park hours are from 8:00 a.m. to 9:00 p.m. June to Sept; 8:00 a.m. to 7:00 p.m. Sept to Nov; 8:00 a.m. to 5:00 p.m. Nov to Mar; and 8:00 a.m. to 7:00 p.m. Mar to June
Trailhead amenities: Ample parking, restrooms, water, and information are available at the trailhead. Visit the museum to pick up (for a fee) the booklet for the self-guided tree tour of the arboretum.
Maps: USGS Reno; wander at will on the arboretum trails, as you cannot get lost.
Trail contacts: Washoe County Department of Regional Parks and Open Space, 2601 Plumas St., Reno 89509; (775) 823-6500; www.washoecountyparks .com. The garden's direct line is (775) 785-4153; the Web site is www.maycenter.com.

Finding the trailhead: The arboretum's address in Rancho San Rafael Regional Park is 1595 N. Sierra St. From I-80 take the down-town Reno/Virginia Street exit. Go north on North Sierra Street for 0.8 mile to Putnam Drive. Go left (west) on Putnam Drive for 0.1 mile to the signed entrance to Rancho San Rafael Regional Park. Follow the park road to the visitor center/museum/arboretum parking areas on the right (northeast). Park near the May Museum and the Wilbur D. May Great Basin Adventure; the signed arboretum entrance is between the two. GPS: N39 32.760' / W119 49.548'

The Hike

Wilbur D. May, whose name graces the arboretum, museum, and Great Basin discovery center in Rancho San Rafael Regional Park, was a polymath who arrived in Reno in 1936. Rancher, artist, sportsman, composer, world traveler, philanthropist—his legacy is preserved in this collection of public treasures.

Though May's name is splashed across this metropolitan park, the land on which the arboretum sits has been utilized or owned by many people, according to park literature. First were the Washoe Indians, the native people that thrived in the fruitful desert and alpine highlands of the region. European ranch owners included the Pincolini brothers, who arrived in 1896, then the Jensen family, and then the Herman family, for whom the pond along the route is named. Products of the ranch helped sustain Reno's casino industry around the turn of the twentieth century. A multifaceted preservation effort that stretched from 1976 to 1979 resulted in what is now one of the most popular regional parks in the Reno area.

The arboretum consists of interwoven trails lined with small gardens. The plants in each garden are meticulously identified and consist of natives and exotics alike. Wander at

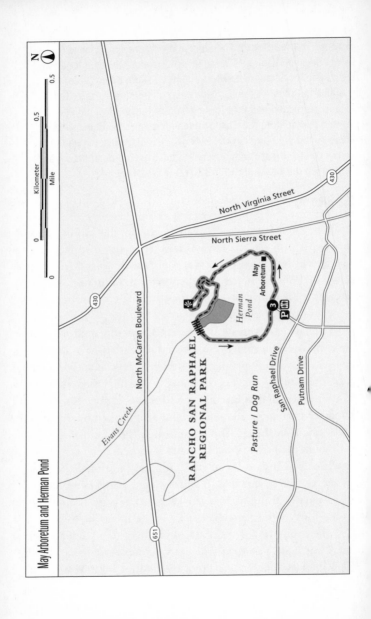

May Arboretum and Herman Pond

N

Kilometer
0   0.5

Mile
0   0.5

430

North Virginia Street

North Sierra Street

430

May
Arboretum

3

P

RANCHO SAN RAPHAEL
REGIONAL PARK

Herman Pond

North McCarran Boulevard

Pasture / Dog Run

San Raphael Drive

Putnam Drive

Evans Creek

651

will; the route described here makes a vague counterclock-wise tour of the gardens, passing willows and pines, snow-berries and roses, sages and oaks, overlooks and gazebos, and shaded benches, nooks, and crannies in xeriscape and cultivation. The gardens are named, providing landmarks, but none is so distant from another that you can get lost.

The high point of the arboretum is the Irwin Overlook, near the Carl Santini garden. Interpretive signs identify the sites: the Virginia Range with notes about its geology and history, including the Comstock Lode; Slide Mountain and Mount Rose; the Carson Range and the Sierra Nevada beyond; Crystal Peak and Peavine Peak to the northwest. Below them all sprawls the Truckee Meadows, with Reno's downtown high-rises front and center.

Drop rather steeply from the overlook in the arboretum to the trail that skirts Herman Pond, a stock pond created by the damming of Evans Creek in 1954. Floods overran the pond twice, in 1986 and 1997—hard to envision from a seat on a waterside bench where you can enjoy the quiet water, the friendly ducks, and views of the Carson Range. The pond is open for fishing, but swimming is not permitted.

Miles and Directions

0.0 Start by heading down the paved path beside the May Museum through the various gardens.

0.2 Drop left (north) to the Evans Creek Bridge and the May Grove. The arboretum paths are paved with decomposed granite on the north side of the bridge.

0.3 Stay on the highest paths to reach Fannie's Garden, then continue up to the Irwin Overlook, where you'll enjoy expansive views and interpretive signs.

0.7 Descend rather steeply from the overlook to the baseline trail and go right (north) toward Herman Pond. The trail circles the pond in a counterclockwise direction.

0.8 Cross the pond's inlet via a boardwalk. At the junction of the Pasture Loop Trail and the Evans Canyon Trail stay left (northwest) on the Evans Canyon Trail, skirting the dog-romping pasture.

1.0 Reach the T junction with the trail into the pooch play area and the arboretum/museum parking area. A park map confirms your location. Go left (southeast) to close the loop.

1.1 Arrive back at the trailhead.

Options: Rancho San Rafael Regional Park offers options galore, though not all of them are for the hiker. The museum houses art galleries and historical displays that include Wilbur May's collections from his world travels. The fenced pasture area attracts a plethora of dogs and their owners. The park is ground zero for the Great Reno Balloon Race. (Children and adults alike will be delighted by the Great Basin Adventure area, complete with log flume rides and a children's petting zoo.) Hikers can also explore the nature trail and Evans Creek, which lie just north of the arboretum at the Reno Sports Complex trailhead.

4 Downtown River Walk

The Truckee River flows right through the glitz of down-town Reno, and the town has dressed up this lovely short promenade along its banks with flowers, sculpture, waterfalls, bridges, and a whitewater park.

Distance: 2 miles out and back, give or take

Approximate hiking time: 1 hour (more or less)

Difficulty: Easy

Trail surface: Pavement

Best seasons: Year-round

Other trail users: Cyclists, trail runners, skaters

Canine compatibility: Leashed dogs permitted

Land status: City of Reno

Fees and permits: None

Schedule: Any time

Trailhead amenities: Parking is available along the road and in Barbara Bennett Park (space permitting). If you begin in Bennett Park, you'll also have easy access to restrooms, information, and the whitewater park.

Maps: USGS Reno; no map is necessary, as the paved trail is well defined.

Trail contacts: City of Reno Parks, Recreation and Community Services Department, 190 E. Liberty St., Reno 89501; (775) 334-6265; www.cityofreno.com

Finding the trailhead: From I-80 take the downtown Reno/Virginia Street exit. Head south on Virginia Street for about 0.5 mile, though downtown, to West Second Street. Go right (west) on Second Street for 2 blocks to North Arlington Avenue. Go left (south) on North Arlington, over the Truckee River, and turn right (west) into signed Barbara Bennett Park. Parking is available on city streets in this area, too. GPS: N39 31.434' / W119 49.019'

The Hike

Even the most dedicated gamer needs a little time away from the tables, and the Truckee River Parkway, tracing the sparkling Truckee adjacent to Reno's casino district, provides a convenient and entertaining diversion.

If you worry you won't be entertained, never fear. The riverside path overflows with people-watching potential. Cyclists, skaters, dog walkers, waders, rafters, kayakers, picnickers, dancing children and swimming teens, basketball players, and dancers, jugglers, and other street performers—they are all here, enjoying the playland that's been built along the water. Perhaps most fun to watch are the kayakers, spinning in the whitewater created by artfully placed rock bars that pinch the river's flow. The kids are fun to watch, too, jumping from the rocks into the water and floating gently downstream . . .

Getting clear of the crowds is as easy as meeting them. A few blocks west of downtown the trail enters a greenbelt through a quiet neighborhood, where friends and lovers rest on painted benches in the shade of spreading cottonwoods to watch the river and admire the impressive homes perched on the high south-side embankment.

There are many ways to access this popular trail—and many ways to enjoy its amenities—so feel free to improvise on the tour described here, which begins in busy Bennett Park on the south side of the river near the whitewater park. Head south to Wingfield Park, an island in the river reached by arcing pedestrian bridges. The park is outfitted with an amphitheater and grassy greens; bright flowers spill from pots on the bridges, and people spill from the edges of the park to dangle their feet in the cooling river.

The trail proper is on the north side of the river, with access to shopping and restaurants as well as the casinos. You can explore in either direction, but be sure to head east (right), crossing the next bridge to the south side of the river (alongside Island Avenue) to the waterfall and sculpture garden. The colorful flowerpots and charming gazebos offer counterpoint to sculptures of eagles, deer, bear, mountain goats, and other creatures showered in sheets of clear water.

You can continue east all the way to Sparks (Reno's sister city), but to reach the greenbelt stretch, circle back to the west at Virginia Street, crossing again to the north side of the river and returning to Wingfield Park. Cross North Arlington Avenue, pausing on the bridge to check out the river antics, then continue west, past little Lunsford Park, into a quiet neighborhood.

The trail is distinctly calmer here, with sturdy cottonwoods spreading shade over a linear green that borders a more natural riparian zone along the riverbanks. The homes on the north side, along Riverside Drive, are modest and charming; the mansions on the south side are to be envied. Benches along the trail look across the river to the palatial houses and their lovely gardens.

Though the trail continues westward toward the Carson Range, a likely turnaround point is the Keystone Avenue Bridge, just beyond the McKinley Arts and Culture Center and interpretive signs about Reno's origins and local arts and culture. Unless you chose to explore farther, retrace your steps from here to the trailhead.

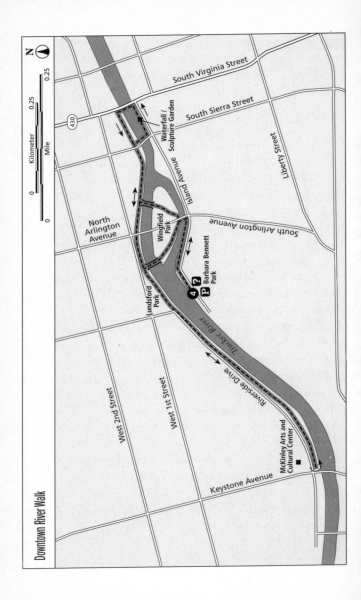

Downtown River Walk

N

0   0.25   Kilometer
0   0.25   Mile

South Virginia Street

South Sierra Street

Waterfall /
Sculpture Garden

430

Island Avenue

South Arlington Avenue

Liberty Street

North
Arlington
Avenue

Wingfield
Park

Barbara Bennett
Park

P

4 2

Lundsford
Park

Truckee River

West 2nd Street

West 1st Street

Riverside Drive

McKinley Arts and
Cultural Center

Keystone Avenue

Miles and Directions

0.0   Start at Bennett Park heading east. Cross the intersection of West First Street and North Arlington Avenue to Wingfield Park.

0.1   Pass an interpretive sign about Reno's origins, then cross the bridge to the south side of the river and explore the waterfall and sculpture garden.

0.4   Circle back to Wingfield Park, cross North Arlington Avenue, and head left (west) on the north side of the river.

0.6   Enter the neighborhoods bordering Riverside Drive.

0.8   Reach the greenbelt section, with benches and views of expensive riverside estates.

1.0   Pass the McKinley Arts and Culture Center before the turn-around point under the Keystone Avenue Bridge. Retrace your steps toward Wingfield Park.

2.0   Arrive back at the Bennett Park trailhead.

Options: The Truckee River Parkway extends for 13 miles and can be picked up at a number of locations within Reno. One option: Extend your walk east from the Reno whitewater park to the whitewater park in neighboring Sparks.

5 Oxbow Nature Study Area Loop

Tour the last pocket of riparian wildland along the sparkling Truckee River within Reno's city limits and witness how nature recovers after fire.

Distance: 1-mile lollipop loop

Approximate hiking time: 45 minutes to 1 hour

Difficulty: Easy

Trail surface: Wide gravel and dirt trail, boardwalk

Best seasons: Year-round

Other trail users: None

Canine compatibility: Dogs not permitted

Land status: City of Reno; Nevada Division of Wildlife

Fees and permits: None

Schedule: Gates open at 8:00 a.m. daily. In winter the park closes at 4:00 p.m.; in summer it closes at sunset. During spring, summer, and fall the interpretive center is open from Mon to Fri from 8:00 a.m. to 5:00 p.m.,

but, according to land managers, there are no guarantees.

Trailhead amenities: You'll find limited parking, restrooms, water, picnic facilities, and an interpretive center at the trailhead.

Maps: USGS Reno; no map is necessary

Trail contacts: City of Reno Parks, Recreation, and Community Services Department, 190 East Liberty St., Reno 89501; (775) 334-2260; www.cityofreno .com. Nevada Department of Wildlife (NDOW), 1100 Valley Rd., Reno 89512; (775) 334-3808; www.ndow.org. The contact number for school groups is (775) 334-3808.

Finding the trailhead: From I-80 just west of downtown Reno take the Keystone Avenue exit. Go left (south) on Keystone Avenue for 0.5 mile to West Second Street. Go right (west) on Second Street for 0.4 mile; it turns into Dickerson Road. Continue another 0.6 mile to the end of Dickerson Road at the park gate. GPS: N39 31.117' / W119 50.774'

The Hike

Flanked by railroad tracks, local businesses, and apartment complexes, the setting for Oxbow Nature Study Area is distinctly urban. But within the park's boundaries, you are insulated from the city by greenery, birdsong, and the soothing rumble of the Truckee River rushing over its rocky bed.

For the next few years, the nature study area will be in a state of transition. A human-caused fire burned about eighteen of the park's twenty-two acres in April 2008, taking out some of the grand old cottonwoods that thrived in the dense riparian zone and the boardwalk and interpretive signs that guided exploration of the area. A new loop trail—bordered by unfinished fences and new plantings still in their protective plastic grow tubes—was in place by spring 2009 and is described here. Visitors, especially as they return over time, will be able to witness the stages of recovery, a fascinating, natural, and generally restorative process for native plants and animals.

Fire is not the only natural force that has transformed Oxbow since it was established in 1991. The dollop of wilderness was flooded in 1997, with boulders, sand, and other debris rushing down the Truckee. According to the interpretive brochure available on the NDOW Web site (outdated since the fire), 5 feet of sand was deposited in the park during that event.

For all the intermittent drama, Oxbow remains a peaceful place. Though charred snags are evident throughout, willows and grasses grow green along the riverbanks. Birds—sparrows, woodpeckers, robins—flit and chit in the brush. If you pass quietly and softly you're likely to see other woodland creatures such as rabbits and squirrels, and you might be treated to a rarer sighting of deer or coyote, a mink or a muskrat.

Begin your tour of the park by reading the informative interpretive signs at the trailhead and checking out the viewing platforms. Climb stairs to an overlook of the Truckee, its riparian corridor, and the small pond that borders the river. Go right (west) on the trail to the pond, where you're sure to see ducks and may also spy a heron or muskrat. Beyond the small picnic green to the left (east) another boardwalk leads out onto the Truckee itself, willows crowding the edges of the cold, rumbling water.

The trail begins at the base of the elevated viewing platform. At the outset there is no sign of fire, but you'll enter the burn zone quickly. Once in the zone, the Truckee (and perhaps a canoe or two) comes into view to the left (south), and the brush thins enough to see the urban borders of the greenbelt, the railroad on one side and apartments across the river on the other.

When the trail splits to form a loop head to the right (northwest); the route is described as a counterclockwise circuit. The path winds through recovering grasslands and burned snags, with willow regaining ground quickly. Meet the wide gravel trail (the return path) at a T junction and walk a bit farther right (west) to explore a small meadow at the park's boundary. Then follow the gravel trail back toward the trailhead. Pass a bench and interpretive sign before following the shoreline of the Truckee to the first trail junction. Retrace your steps from the trail split to the trailhead.

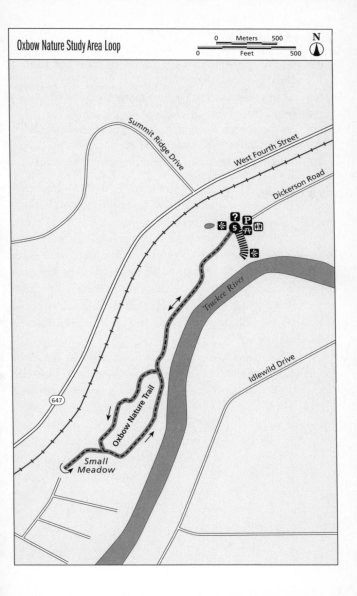

Oxbow Nature Study Area Loop

0   Meters   500
0   Feet   500

N

Summit Ridge Drive

West Fourth Street

Dickerson Road

Truckee River

Idlewild Drive

647

Oxbow Nature Trail

Small
Meadow

Miles and Directions

0.0 Start by visiting the viewing platforms and pond, then set off down the signed main trail.

0.3 Go right (northwest) on the fenced trail through the meadow.

0.5 Meet a wide gravel path (the return route). Go right (west) into the meadow at the park's edge, then return to the trail junction and go right, following the gravel track.

0.75 Reach the first trail junction; stay right (straight) to retrace your steps to the trailhead.

1.0 Arrive back at the trailhead.

6 Verdi Nature Trail

The steep Sierran canyon that restrains the Truckee River opens up at Verdi, and this nature trail, an educational gem for schoolchildren and adults alike, explores the unique environment of this foothills transition zone.

Distance: 0.5-mile loop
Approximate hiking time: 45 minutes
Difficulty: Easy
Trail surface: Dirt and decomposed gravel singletrack
Best seasons: Year-round
Other trail users: None
Canine compatibility: Leashed dogs permitted
Land status: Nevada Division of Wildlife
Fees and permits: None
Schedule: Sunrise to sunset
Trailhead amenities: The trailhead is located in the parking lot of the Verdi Community Library and Wildlife Education Center, where you'll find information and restrooms (when open). There is ample parking, trash cans, and information (including interpretive guides) at the trailhead.
Maps: USGS Verdi; the interpretive guide at the trailhead also has a map
Trail contacts: Nevada Division of Wildlife (NDOW), 1100 Valley Rd., Reno 89512; (775) 334-3808; www.ndow.org
Other: The Verdi Community Library and Wildlife Education Center is open on Tues and Thurs from 3:00 to 7:00 p.m., and on Sat from 10:00 a.m. to 4:00 p.m. It is closed Mon, Wed, Fri, and Sun.

Finding the trailhead: From I-80 westbound take the first Verdi exit (exit 5). Follow the frontage road to the traffic circle, then merge onto Old US 40. Follow US 40 west for about 2.3 miles to Bridge Street in "downtown" Verdi. Turn right (north) on Bridge Street and go 0.2 mile to the signed Verdi Community Library parking lot on the right (east). The address is 270 Bridge St. The well-signed trailhead is on the north side of the parking lot. GPS: N39 31.309' / W119 59.446'

The Hike

This little loop is about as charming as a day hike can be. Much like the schoolchildren it caters to, the trail is sweet, honest, and playful . . . and also spiced with surprises that are best appreciated when you walk slowly and carry the interpretive guide keyed to signposts along the track. Couple the hike with a picnic in nearby Crystal Peak Regional Park (a Washoe County park) on the banks of the Truckee River for a great family outing.

Though the trail is scenic, perched on a flat shelf just above the Truckee with views across the river valley into the evergreen foothills of Humboldt-Toiyabe National Forest, the setting is more complex than its simple beauty might imply. The path circles through the transition zone between the lower montane region of the Sierra Nevada, dominated by Jeffrey and ponderosa pine woodlands, and the high desert of the Great Basin, where desert peach, bitterbrush, and sagebrush vie for dominance. Concise descriptions of the flora and the fauna (such as coyote, mule deer, and western fence lizards) are interspersed with more general observations about the geology and geography of the area. Human history is also touched upon, with mention of an old flume that funneled water out of the neighboring schoolyard, once a refreshing place for summer play.

The route begins behind the signboard, which notes that volunteers built the trail in 1998. Pass under the power lines; the interpretive stops come in quick succession. A bench at post 6 offers a place to catch up. The trail bumps up against itself near Storyteller's Rock (at post 8); stay left

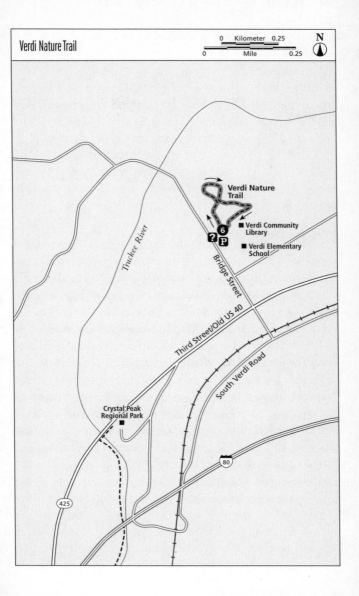

Verdi Nature Trail

0 Kilometer 0.25
0 Mile 0.25

N

Verdi Nature Trail

6 P

?

Verdi Community Library

Verdi Elementary School

Truckee River

Bridge Street

Third Street/Old US 40

South Verdi Road

Crystal Peak Regional Park

80

425

(north) to round the loop in a clockwise direction, passing an interpretive sign about how different animals survive the winter months.

Drop down a short series of steps into a meadowland where the trail is lined with timbers and where you'll find another bench. The natural area is separated from the Truckee's gorge by a neighboring golf course and a fence.

Climb back into the sage as you circle to the south. Posts with arrows are interspersed with the interpretive posts, keeping you on track. The last few posts bend west as you return to the trailhead.

Miles and Directions

0.0 Start.

0.1 The outbound part of the loop trail bumps up against the returning section; stay left (north) to post 8 at Storyteller's Rock.

0.3 Pass a bench and an interpretive sign about animal tracks and forage.

0.5 Arrive back at the trailhead.

Options: Crystal Peak Regional Park is just upstream on the Truckee and offers picnic facilities, restrooms, river access, and informal trails along the riverbanks. From the Verdi Nature Trail, return to Old US 40 (Third Street) and go right (west) to Crystal Peak Road. Turn left (southwest) on Crystal Peak Road and follow it about 0.2 mile to the signed park entrance on the right (west).

7 Hole in the Wall

Contrary to the lore of the Wild West, Reno's Hole in the Wall is not an outlaw hideout. This is literally a hole in a rock wall: a narrow tunnel gushing snowmelt into Steamboat Ditch. The route to the hole begins alongside the cooling flow of the Truckee River, then climbs to an easy walk along the ditch with views in all directions.

Distance: 5.6 miles out and back

Approximate hiking time: 3 hours

Difficulty: More challenging due to length, steep pitches, and lack of shade

Trail surface: Paved bike path, dirt singletrack, dirt roadway

Best seasons: Winter, spring, and fall; avoid this trail on hot days, as it is completely exposed to the desert sun.

Other trail users: Mountain bikers, equestrians, trail runners

Canine compatibility: Leashed dogs permitted (but be warned: many run free)

Land status: Mayberry Park; Truckee River Parkway West; public and private land

Fees and permits: None

Schedule: Mayberry Park is open from 8:00 a.m. to 9:00 p.m.

June to Sept; 8:00 a.m. to 7:00 p.m. Sept to Nov; 8:00 a.m. to 5:00 p.m. Nov to Mar; and 8:00 a.m. to 7:00 p.m. Mar to June

Trailhead amenities: Though there are plenty of spaces in the paved lot at Mayberry Park, these fill quickly on warm spring and summer weekends. The park also has restrooms, trash cans, picnic greens and tables, and easy river access.

Maps: USGS Verdi, Mount Rose NW; www.nvtrailmaps.com

Trail contacts: Mayberry Park is managed by the Washoe County Department of Regional Parks and Open Space, 2601 Plumas St., Reno 89509; (775) 823-6500; www.washoecountyparks .com. Other trail segments are maintained by City of Reno Parks, Recreation, & Community Services, 190 E. Liberty St.,

Reno 89501; (775) 334-2260; www.cityofreno.com.

Special considerations: The Steamboat Ditch Trail crosses private property, so remain on the well-used dirt track. Social paths intersecting the Tom Cooke Trail should be avoided, because shortcutting causes erosion, degrades the environment, and creates unsightly scars on the landscape.

Other: Mayberry Park is often crowded in spring, summer, and fall. Parking can be difficult; a second lot is east of the main lot down the dirt road.

Finding the trailhead: From I-80 westbound from Reno, take the West McCarran Boulevard exit. Go left (south) on West McCarran for 0.7 mile to West Fourth Street. Turn right (west) on West Fourth Street and travel 1.9 miles to Woodland Avenue. Turn left (south) and follow Woodland Avenue for 0.4 mile to its end in a driveway between warehouses; the driveway leads into Mayberry Park and to the Truckee River Parkway. GPS: N30 30.155' / W119 53.844'

The Hike

Linking the Truckee River Parkway, the Tom Cooke Trail, and the Steamboat Ditch Trail offers a snapshot tour of the area's premier riparian corridor, a long exploration of the scenic high desert landscapes of the lower Carson Range, and vistas of Peavine Peak and the Truckee Meadows.

The route begins in the shade of stately cottonwoods along the Truckee River in Mayberry Park, which on hot summer days is inundated with families and young people carrying tubes and small rafts. Dirt tracks lead to narrow beaches along the river where the floaters put in or where picnic blankets may be spread.

The paved parkway leads right (west) along the river's bottomlands, with warehouses bordering on the right (north) and steep, undeveloped canyon walls on the left (south). The pavement ends behind the Patagonia warehouse at a metal bridge and a rustic picnic shelter. Crossing the bridge is a bit exciting (especially for kids and dogs), as you can look down onto the swift flow of the water through the planks of the span.

On the south side of the river climb up to the left (southwest) to a wooden footbridge over the Last Chance Ditch. Like the Steamboat Ditch, which rides the hillsides above, the Last Chance carries Sierra snowmelt to thirsty high desert ranches. The signed Tom Cooke Trail begins on the south side of the ditch.

The well-built singletrack uses switchbacks to climb a steep, rocky cleft in the scrub-covered hillside. Practice good stewardship of the open space by avoiding the social routes carved by careless hikers and cyclists.

The Tom Cooke Trail tops out on an open hillside with views up and across the grass and sage-covered foothills of the Carson Range. Look north across the Truckee River valley to Peavine Peak. Subdivisions and business parks fill the valley itself, and the whistle of a passing train (along with highway noise from the adjacent interstate) may waft up to the vista point, but Peavine Mountain behind is relatively unscarred.

The Tom Cooke Trail widens to double track as it climbs to the Steamboat Ditch Trail. At the T intersection with the ditch trail, go right (west) on the obvious, well-used dirt roadway, which you'll follow all the way to the Hole in the Wall.

Steamboat Ditch, completed in the early 1880s, funnels Truckee River water from the Sierra in Verdi down to ranches and farms on the dry desert flatlands before empty-

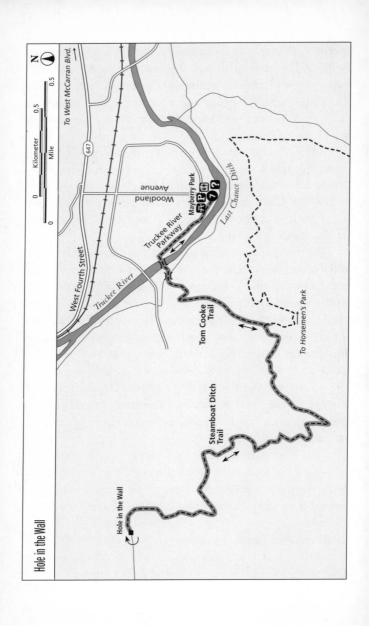

Hole in the Wall

ing back into the Truckee again. It stretches for about 47 miles, and sections of the dirt roadway that parallels it are very popular with hikers, mountain bikers, and trail runners. The Steamboat Ditch Company maintains the ditch itself; the trail crosses private land but has been in public use for so long you won't see a fence or sign noting boundaries. Still, some public land managers are uncomfortable with public use for obvious (and unfortunate) liability issues. Efforts are underway to formalize public access to the entire trail. In the meantime trail lovers continue to follow the ditch, enjoying a distinctive stripe of riparian greenery on the otherwise scrubby mountainsides.

Traverse several gullies as you wind westward along the ditch, climbing so gently you'll hardly notice. As you wind in and out, you'll be treated to different views, sometimes of the Truckee River valley and Peavine, sometimes of the Reno skyline and the distant blue gray ranges of the Great Basin, sometimes of the wooded heights of the Carson Range. An occasional diversion gate marks the head of a ravine.

As you approach the Hole in the Wall, pass a lone pine tree. The trail funnels through a cut in the yellow and brown hillside, then through a spindly bower of shade trees to where, in spring and early summer, water froths into the ditch through the Hole in the Wall. Though other, unsigned trails continue into the hills from this point, this is the end of this leg of the Steamboat Ditch Trail and the turnaround point. Retrace your steps to the trailhead.

Miles and Directions

0.0 Start on the paved Truckee River Parkway heading right (west).

0.3 Cross the bridge to the south side of the Truckee, then bear left (southwest) to cross the Last Chance Ditch and arrive at the signed start of the Tom Cooke Trail.

0.7 Reach the top of the climb at a vista point.

0.9 Arrive at the T junction with the Steamboat Ditch Trail. Go right (west) on the dirt roadway; the ditch trail also branches left (east) toward Reno.

1.4 Curl through a gully with a ditch gate.

2.3 Reach the junction with a dirt road leading right (north) away from the ditch. Stay left (southwest) on the obvious ditch trail. Less than 0.1 mile farther, cross a concrete diversion dam/gate in a gully.

2.5 Pass a lone pine.

2.8 Arrive at the Hole in the Wall and turnaround point.

5.6 Arrive back at the Mayberry Park trailhead.

Option: From the junction of the Tom Cooke Trail and the Steamboat Ditch Trail you can head left (east) to Horseman's Park, where you'll find another trailhead with parking.

8 Dorostkar Park Nature Trail

Coupled with a short stretch of the Truckee River Parkway West, this pleasant nature trail provides an easy outing for river lovers, dog walkers, and families.

Distance: 1.4-mile lollipop loop

Approximate hiking time: 1 hour

Difficulty: Easy

Trail surface: Decomposed granite pathway, dirt singletrack, paved bike path

Best seasons: Year-round, but the route may be uncomfortably hot at midday in summer

Other trail users: Cyclists, trail runners

Canine compatibility: Leashed dogs permitted

Land status: Dorostkar Park

Fees and permits: None

Schedule: The park is open from 8:00 a.m. to 9:00 p.m. June to Sept; 8:00 a.m. to 7:00 p.m. Sept to Nov; 8:00 a.m. to 5:00 p.m. Nov to Mar; and 8:00 a.m. to 7:00 p.m. Mar to June

Trailhead amenities: The small paved parking area holds about twenty cars; there also are picnic tables and trash cans at the trailhead.

Maps: USGS Verdi; no map is necessary as the trail is well defined with interpretive panels.

Trail contacts: Washoe County Department of Regional Parks and Open Space, 2601 Plumas St., Reno 89509; (775) 823-6500; www.washoecounty parks.com

Finding the trailhead: From I-80 westbound take the West McCarran Boulevard exit. Go left (south) on West McCarran for 0.7 mile to West Fourth Street. Turn right (west) on West Fourth Street and travel 1.8 miles to Mayberry Drive. Turn left (south) on Mayberry Drive and go 0.4 mile to the signed park entrance on the left (north). GPS: N39 30.373' / W119 53.192'

The Hike

The cold, clear Truckee River again serves as the center-piece of an easy scenic trek. Interpretive signs punctuate the riparian and high desert habitats traversed by the route, a rich and colorful ecotone that blooms with wild rose and desert peach in spring and early summer.

Begin by crossing the paved Truckee River Parkway and a little bridge over the ditch into the Truckee's narrow riparian zone. Head right (east) where the trail splits, walking downstream between the river and the ditch. Social paths drop left (north) to riverside, but the trail proper stays right, a clear path through a thicket of willow, wild rose, sage, mullein, chicory, soaproot, and other native and invasive species. Read the interpretive signs to learn more about the plants and their uses, as well as about birds, bugs, and land stewardship.

In addition to being in the natural transition zone, the trail also runs through a human-created transition, as it presently sits at the western boundary of suburban Reno. Though the tangle of plants and the constant flow of the Truckee act as a buffer, railroad tracks run along the north side of the river, with train whistles and the thunder of an iron horse's wheels on the rails sometimes intruding on an otherwise peaceful setting. Homes and roadways also nestle against the park.

Leave the riparian zone via a bridge over the ditch at an interpretive sign about animal tracks. Now in the shadeless high desert, the trail splits; continue left (east) on the track that leads up to the paved Truckee River Parkway spur (the nature trail/return route goes right/west). Cross the

Truckee on a substantial pedestrian bridge, with the river flowing fast and blue below. On the north side of the river, the trail passes a small, charming ranch house then curves eastward, parallel to the railroad tracks. The spur ends at a lonely picnic table, with dirt paths leading into the cotton-woods and willows alongside the river. Picnic and explore, then return as you came to the junction with the nature trail to complete a counterclockwise circuit.

The nature trail proceeds through desert scrub. Cross the Truckee River Parkway, which runs parallel to Mayberry Drive on the left (south), then head west on high ground overlooking the river valley. Willow encroaches on the trail as you approach the trailhead, but the way back to the parking area is clear and easy.

Miles and Directions

0.0 Start at the NATURE TRAIL sign by the split rail fence. Cross the Truckee River Parkway. At the T junction go right (east) on the dirt singletrack.

0.4 Cross the bridge over the ditch to a trail junction. Go left (east) on the dirt trail to the Truckee River Parkway spur. Go left (north) on the paved trail, crossing the pedestrian bridge spanning the Truckee.

0.7 Reach the end of the spur trail at a picnic table. Retrace your steps to the nature trail.

1.0 Arrive back at the nature loop and stay left (west) on the path through the desert scrub.

1.2 Cross the Truckee River Parkway. Trail signs and a split-rail fence mark the continuation of the nature trail; stay right (west) where the dirt path splits.

1.4 Arrive back at the trailhead.

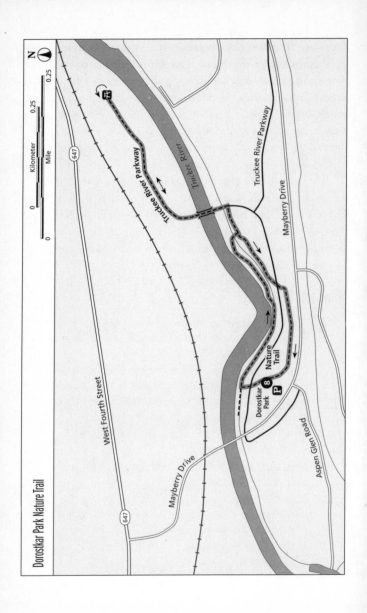

Dorostkar Park Nature Trail

N

Kilometer
0   0.25

Mile
0   0.25

West Fourth Street

647

Mayberry Drive

Truckee River Parkway

Truckee River

Truckee River Parkway

Mayberry Drive

Nature Trail

Dorostkar Park

P 8

Aspen Glen Road

Options: The Truckee River Parkway connects Dorostkar Park and Mayberry Park—an easy, paved alternative or extension. From the trailhead go left (west) on the pavement, passing under the Mayberry bridge and curling south to Aspen Glen Drive. A sign designates the roadway as a pedestrian link to Mayberry Park.

9 Bartley Ranch Regional Park Loop

Well-preserved remnants of Nevada's ranching heritage enliven this suburban trail, with a charming one-room schoolhouse at the trailhead and interpretive panels describing the farm equipment displayed along the latter part of the loop.

Distance: 1.5-mile loop
Approximate hiking time: 1 hour
Difficulty: Moderate due to short steep pitches and changing trail surfaces
Trail surface: Dirt, gravel, a short section of wooden flume
Best seasons: Spring, fall, and winter
Other trail users: None on the Quail Run and Flume Trails; equestrians and mountain bikers on the Ranch Loop Trail
Canine compatibility: Leashed dogs permitted
Land status: Bartley Ranch Regional Park
Fees and permits: None
Schedule: The park is open from 8:00 a.m. to 9:00 p.m. June to Sept; 8:00 a.m. to 7:00 p.m. Sept to Nov; 8:00 a.m. to 5:00 p.m. Nov to Mar; and 8:00 a.m. to 7:00 p.m. Mar to June

Trailhead amenities: You'll find restrooms, water, and picnic facilities at the trailhead.
Maps: USGS Mount Rose NE; a nice map is posted on the exterior wall of the information center; www.nvtrailmaps.com
Trail contacts: Washoe County Department of Regional Parks and Open Space, 2601 Plumas St., Reno 89509; (775) 823-6500; www.washoecountyparks .com. The park's direct line is (775) 828-6612.
Other: Park facilities, including the Old Huffaker Schoolhouse, the Western Heritage Interpretive Center, and the amphitheater, can be rented for private functions. Equestrian arenas are also available. Contact the park for more information.

Finding the trailhead: From US 395 southbound, take the Kietzke Lane exit (exit 63). Stay left, following Kietzke Lane for 0.1 mile to South McCarran Boulevard. Turn right (west) on South McCarran Boulevard and continue for 0.7 mile to Lakeside Drive. Go left (south) on Lakeside Drive for 0.4 mile to Bartley Ranch Road on the left (east). Follow Bartley Ranch Road for about 0.1 mile to the park entrance at the covered bridge. Park in the first lot, for the Old Huffaker Schoolhouse. The trailhead is next to the restrooms. The park address is 6000 Bartley Ranch Rd. GPS: N39 28.125' / W119 48.424'

The Hike

A pocket of ranch land surrounded by Reno's southern suburbs, Bartley Ranch is home to a cluster of interlocking trails that wind through native scrub, along irrigation ditches, and past preserved pieces of farm machinery. The loop, though never far from homes and highway noise, does a good job of evoking Reno's frontier days by showcasing remnants of the past, including a covered flume and the perfectly restored Old Huffaker Schoolhouse. Take a peek inside the schoolhouse if it's open. Clean and well lit, with old-style desks and a glowing wooden floor, the building gives the impression of having absorbed sunshine and the laughter of children into its yellow-painted walls.

Begin on the Quail Run Nature Trail, which meanders through fragrant desert scrub and across several small wooden plank bridges to picnic sites fronting the Western Heritage Interpretive Center. Interpretive posts line the nature trail, but they were blank in spring 2009. The Virginia Range forms a backdrop to equestrian facilities and the Hawkins Amphitheater as you continue.

A short gentle climb leads to the Flume Trail; the neighboring Ranch Loop Trail rides the hillside above. Part of the Flume Trail is built on solid planks silvered by weather covering the Last Chance Ditch. When the "boardwalk" ends, dirt singletrack parallels the ditch, squirreling through the sparse shade of willows and piñon pines nurtured by the greenish brown water.

The Flume Trail ends on the Ranch Loop Trail, where a bridge spans the ditch. Follow the Ranch Loop, which switchbacks downhill to the Anderson Trail and past the end of the Quail Run Trail before skimming the fence lines of neighboring private pastures. Rusting farm implements—a wagon frame from Reno's Flindt Ranch, a hay loader, rakes, a Jackson fork with a Mormon hay derrick, a manure spreader—line the route, and interpretive signs provide information on their origins.

Toward trail's end the Ranch Loop arcs west toward the interpretive center and Old Huffaker Schoolhouse, skirting an adjacent neighborhood park (with a tot lot), and the modern Huffaker Elementary School. Views west climb over adjacent development to the high peaks of the Carson Range, snow-capped in winter and spring.

Miles and Directions

0.0 Start at the signed trailhead for the Quail Run Nature Trail and the Ranch Loop Trail. Climb three steps and go immediately left (southeast) on the Quail Run Nature Trail.

0.1 Stay right (south) on the Quail Run Nature Trail where a side trail drops to the interpretive center. Cross the ditch to another trail crossing, again staying right (up and south) on the Quail Run Nature Trail.

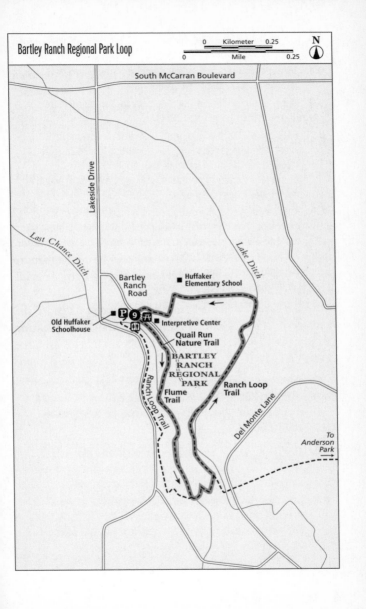

Bartley Ranch Regional Park Loop

South McCarran Boulevard

Lakeside Drive

Last Chance Ditch

Lake Ditch

Bartley Ranch Road

Huffaker Elementary School

Old Huffaker Schoolhouse

P **9**

Interpretive Center

Quail Run Nature Trail

BARTLEY RANCH REGIONAL PARK

Ranch Loop Trail

Flume Trail

Ranch Loop Trail

Del Monte Lane

To Anderson Park

Kilometer 0.25

Mile 0.25

N

0.3 Reach the junction with the Flume Trail. Go right (south) on the wooden planks.

0.5 Meet the Ranch Loop Trail at the end of the Flume Trail. Go left (east) over the bridge on the Ranch Loop Trail.

0.6 Arrive at the Anderson Trail intersection and stay left (north) on the Ranch Loop Trail (BR 4).

0.7 Pass the end of the Quail Run Nature Trail, staying right (north) on the Ranch Loop Trail, toward a fenced pasture. At the next Ranch Loop Trail junction, about 50 yards beyond at the fence and wagon frame, stay right again, passing a hay loader alongside the Lake Ditch.

1.0 At an unmarked trail junction amid a collection of ranching machinery (including the Jackson fork), stay right (north) and circle through a picnic area. The left-hand trail leads toward the riding ring. About 100 yards farther, a trail sign points you right (north), through a dry streambed, to a T junction. Go left (west), alongside a wire fence.

1.2 A paved path leads right (north) into an adjacent neighborhood park. Stay straight (west) on the Ranch Loop Trail.

1.3 A second trail breaks right (north) onto the fenced school property; the equestrian parking area is on the left (south). Bear left (southwest) across the lot, then across a bridge, to the Western Heritage Interpretive Center. Turn right (west), crossing another small parking lot at a covered picnic area to a gravel path that leads back toward the schoolhouse and trailhead.

1.5 Cross the main park road and follow the gravel path back to the trailhead.

10 Lakeview Loop

Expansive views open across the Truckee Meadows to the summits of Mount Rose and Slide Mountain from an easy trail that loops through former ranchland in the distinctive Huffaker Hills.

Distance: 0.9-mile loop

Approximate hiking time: 45 minutes

Difficulty: Easy

Trail surface: Rocky dirt single-track

Best seasons: Winter, spring, and fall

Other trail users: Mountain bikers, equestrians

Canine compatibility: Leashed dogs permitted

Land status: Huffaker Hills Trailhead

Fees and permits: None

Schedule: The park is open from 8:00 a.m. to 9:00 p.m. June to Sept; 8:00 a.m. to 7:00 p.m. Sept to Nov; 8:00 a.m. to 5:00 p.m. Nov to Mar; and 8:00 a.m. to 7:00 p.m. Mar to June

Trailhead amenities: You'll find a paved parking lot, picnic tables, a restroom, and an information billboard with trail map at the trailhead.

Maps: USGS Steamboat; www.nvtrailmaps.com (Huffaker Lookout)

Trail contacts: Washoe County Department of Regional Parks and Open Space, 2601 Plumas St., Reno 89509; (775) 823-6500; www.washoecountyparks.com

Special considerations: The trails are completely shadeless and oven hot on summer days.

Finding the trailhead: From US 395 southbound take the Kietske Lane/South Virginia Street exit. Go left (south) on Kietske Lane for 0.1 mile to South McCarran Boulevard. Turn left (east) on South McCarran Boulevard and go 1.6 miles, past the signal at Longley Lane, to Alexander Lake Road (just behind the shopping center). Turn right (south) on Alexander Lake Road and go 1 mile up to the signed trailhead and parking area on the right (west). GPS: N39 27.995' / W119 45.228'

The Hike

Slide Mountain and Mount Rose form a stony backdrop to the softer browns of the Twin Peaks as you set off on this rocky desert trail. The Truckee Meadows, silver and green with development and greenbelts, fill the gap between the two sets of summits, and to the northwest the towers of Reno's casino district rise up before the base of massive Peavine Peak.

The trails of Huffaker Hills lie on the former ranch of Granville Huffaker, according to park literature. Huffaker homesteaded here in 1859 with 500 head of cattle destined to feed miners toiling in nearby Virginia City. From a gritty start in a dugout cave at the base of the hills, Huffaker eventually came to own a mansion, a railroad and Pony Express station, a post office, and a store. The interpretive signboard at the trailhead details Huffaker's accomplishments and describes the cooperative effort that led to preservation of the land.

Pass the information signboard on the merged Lakeview and Western Loops; the trails split at an interpretive sign. Head left (south) on the Lakeview Loop, traveling in a counterclockwise direction.

The stark, water-challenged landscape supports only stunted desert scrub, which permits uninterrupted views of the Carson Range and Truckee Meadows. The park is also below the flight path of planes taking off and landing at Reno International Airport; as much as this is a distraction from the natural world, it also adds a bit of spice to a hike here, especially for kids.

As the trail continues south and the Twin Peaks block Sierra vistas, new views open into the dry Virginia Range to the left (east). Along this stretch you'll pass an interpretive marker that describes the Great Basin blooms of springtime, including mariposa lily and prickly pear. Several other interpretive signs line the trail loop as well.

The trail to Twin Peaks breaks off to the right (southwest), while the Lakeview Trail continues southeast past the sun-bleached trail sign. A fenced-off pea-soup green reservoir nudges into view as the trail begins to gently descend, with the junction to the reservoir overlook following in short order.

The short spur to the reservoir overlook ends at a bench installed by a local Eagle Scout, where you can pause to contemplate the lake, its concrete dam, and the parched Virginia Range behind. On a hot day the water is deliciously tempting . . . if the chain-link fencing isn't enough of a deterrent, knowing that the reservoir holds treated effluent should keep you clear . . .

Back at the trail junction stay right (downhill and north), following the fence line before beginning the short climb through broken rocks and scrub to the trailhead.

Miles and Directions

0.0   Start on the combined Lakeview and Western Loop trails. The paths split about 25 yards beyond the trailhead at an interpretive signboard; stay left (south) on the Lakeview Loop.

0.3   Pass the junction with the Twin Peaks Trail on the right (southwest); remain left (southeast) on Lakeview Trail.

0.4   Arrive at the junction with the spur trail to the reservoir and go right (southeast) on the spur.

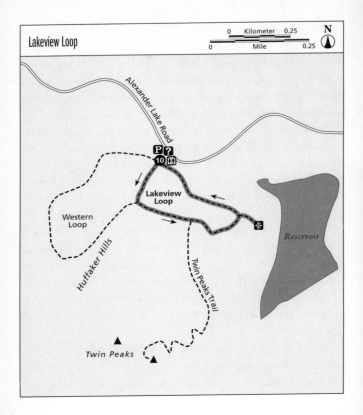

Lakeview Loop

0 Kilometer 0.25
0 Mile 0.25

N

Alexander Lake Road

P
10
?

Lakeview
Loop

Western
Loop

Huffaker Hills

Twin Peaks Trail

Reservoir

Twin Peaks

0.5 Reach the reservoir overlook and bench.

0.6 Back at the spur trail junction stay right (north) on the continuation of the Lakeview Loop.

0.9 Descend along the fence line and climb past the park's picnic tables back to the trailhead.

Options: If you have the time and inclination, you can add the Western Loop and the out-and-back leg of the Twin Peaks Trail to your tour of Huffaker Hills Trailhead.

Other east-side trailheads can be found at nearby Washoe County's Hidden Valley Regional Park and Huffaker Park. Trails currently aren't marked at Hidden Valley, making it a bit of a route-finding experiment. Huffaker Park, a City of Reno park on Offenhauser Drive, offers another looping tour of the Huffaker Hills, with a gazebo offering a great place to take in the views. The park also has inviting trailhead amenities, including picnic areas and a tot lot.

11 South Meadows Trail

A spread of wetland preserved among South Valley subdivisions anchors the South Meadows Trail, part of an urban trail system linking residents and visitors with parks, schools, shopping, and natural areas.

Distance: 1.4 miles out and back

Approximate hiking time: 1 hour

Difficulty: Easy

Trail surface: Smooth pavement

Best seasons: Year-round; there is little shade along this section of trail, so avoid the heat of the day in summer.

Other trail users: Cyclists, trail runners, skaters

Canine compatibility: Leashed dogs permitted

Land status: City of Reno

Fees and permits: None

Schedule: Sunrise to sunset

Trailhead amenities: The trailhead is at Evergreen Park and the Double Diamond Elementary School. Parking is plentiful, trash cans are provided, and there's a large lawn for rest and relaxation.

Maps: USGS Mount Rose NE; downloadable map at www .nvtrailmaps.com

Trail contacts: City of Reno Parks, Recreation, & Community Services Department, 190 E. Liberty St., Reno 89501; (775) 334-2260; www.cityofreno.com

Finding the trailhead: From US 395 southbound, take the South Meadows Parkway exit. Go left (east) on South Meadows Parkway for about 0.8 mile to Evergreen Street on the right (south), at Double Diamond Elementary School. Follow Evergreen Street to the parking lot behind the school for Evergreen Park. Trailhead GPS: N39 26.403'/ W119 44.786'

The Hike

One of the greatest challenges facing urban planners in a fast-growing metropolitan area like Reno is ensuring ample access to open spaces and parks. Urban trails, like those in South Meadows and other developing sections of the city, are part of the green and health-minded movement toward pedestrian-friendly neighborhoods that allow residents and visitors to walk or bicycle between shopping centers, schools, parks, and public transportation. The City of Reno and other public entities are rightly proud of their efforts to ensure new subdivisions and commercial developments are outfitted with useful trail links.

This section of the evolving South Meadows Trail System skirts a wetland on the south side of Whites Creek. It's bounded on all sides by subdivisions but still boasts views of Mount Rose, Slide Mountain, and the Virginia Range. The wetland supports habitat for a variety of urban wildlife, including rabbits and red-winged blackbirds. Cattails and reeds maintain a foothold in the center of the marsh, but the invasive weed commonly called whitetop clots the rim; the flowers are pretty but they've become a plague on Nevada's rangelands.

The trail is well maintained and nicely manicured, with open fencing, gated links to residential streets, benches overlooking the wetland set in the shade of fledgling trees, and trash containers. The path is handicapped accessible and perfect for families, dog walkers, runners, and cyclists.

Traveling this section is straightforward. Begin on the paved path in the southeast corner of the parking area and head right (southwest). The wetland sprawls southward, with the route hugging the northern boundary and the

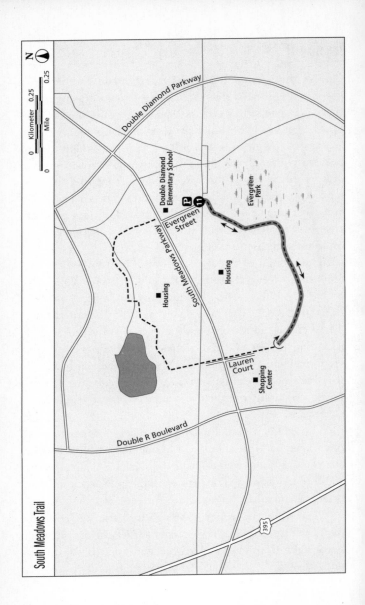

South Meadows Trail

fenced separation from adjacent development. Loop westward, enjoying views up toward Mount Rose and Slide Mountain as you continue to trail's end at a shopping center off of Lauren Court. You can link to other paved trails in the area via sidewalks; otherwise turn around here and retrace your steps to the trailhead.

Miles and Directions

0.0   Start at the southeast corner of the parking lot and go right (southwest) on the paved trail.

0.7   Reach the end of the paved section of trail at Lauren Court; this is the turnaround point.

1.4   Arrive back at the trailhead.

Options: You can make a loop by linking this section of trail with neighborhood streets and the path around a pretty pond on the north side of South Meadows Parkway. Follow Lauren Court to the crosswalk on the parkway; on the north side of the road, an unpaved trail crisscrossed by BMX tracks links to the paved trail around the pond. Go right (east) on the trail to where it ends on sidewalk adjacent to residences, then follow residential streets back south to the trailhead.

Another subdivision with an extensive urban trail system worth exploring is in Somersett, on the lower slopes of Peavine Peak in west Reno. Contact the City of Reno parks department for more information.

12 Lower Whites Creek Trail

Tucked in a ravine surrounded by subdivisions, the riparian habitat supported by the lower reaches of Whites Creek envelopes you in an unexpected, if narrowly defined, desert wilderness.

Distance: 2.8 miles out and back
Approximate hiking time: 2 hours
Difficulty: Moderate due to trail length and steady incline
Trail surface: Dirt singletrack
Best seasons: Winter, spring, and late fall; avoid the heat of the day in summer
Other trail users: Mountain bikers, equestrians (no horse trailer parking), trail runners
Canine compatibility: Leashed dogs permitted
Land status: Whites Creek Park
Fees and permits: None
Schedule: Whites Creek Park is open from 8:00 a.m. to 9:00 p.m. June to Sept; 8:00 a.m. to 7:00 p.m. Sept to Nov; 8:00 a.m. to 5:00 p.m. Nov to Mar; and 8:00 a.m. to 7:00 p.m. Mar to June
Trailhead amenities: You'll find a generous parking area, a tot lot, picnic facilities, and a fenced playing field near the trailhead.
Maps: USGS Mount Rose NE; downloadable map at www .nvtrailmaps.com
Trail contacts: Washoe County Department of Regional Parks and Open Space, 2601 Plumas St., Reno 89509; (775) 823-6500; www.washoecountyparks.com

Finding the trailhead: From US 395 southbound, take the NV 431 (Mount Rose Highway) exit. Follow Mount Rose Highway west for 2 miles to Telluride Drive (the second Galena Country Estates turnoff). Turn right (north) on Telluride Drive and go 0.2 mile to Killington Drive. Turn left (west) on Killington Drive; the road ends in 0.2 mile at Whites Creek Park. Continue on the unpaved park road for 0.1 mile, past the fenced field, to the parking area at the trailhead. GPS: N39 23.786' / W119 47.980'

The Hike

The winding singletrack that follows Whites Creek through subdivisions at the foot of Mount Rose is the perfect quick escape. Whether you've got time before work, after work, or between soccer games on a Saturday afternoon, a hike on the creekside trail will soothe your senses and invigorate your body.

The route begins in a dense riparian strip. Of all the foliage springing up on either side of the stream, perhaps the most striking are the aspens, with electric green leaves in springtime changing to wedding-ring gold in autumn. Wildflowers (notably pretty pink wild rose), stately cottonwoods, and tangles of willow clutter the banks of the stream; the drier slopes of the gully walls are cloaked in desert scrub, and ringing the shallow canyon on either side are neighborhood homes, their backyards sloping steeply to meet the creek.

The route boasts views too—of Mount Rose and the lower peaks of the Carson Range as you travel westward, and of the southern reaches of the Truckee Meadows narrowing between the dry hills rimming the South Valley on the return trip.

The trail starts on the south side of the stream—a boisterous companion in spring and early summer that dwindles in summer and fall—but within the first 0.5-mile crosses to the north side via either of a pair of small wooden bridges. Social trails on the south side can be distracting: If you begin a decent climb that tops out on a neighborhood road, simply descend and backtrack to the first bridge you reach.

Once on the north side of the creek, you'll climb steadily toward the mountains, sometimes tucked in a riparian veil that hides the houses on either side. There's no

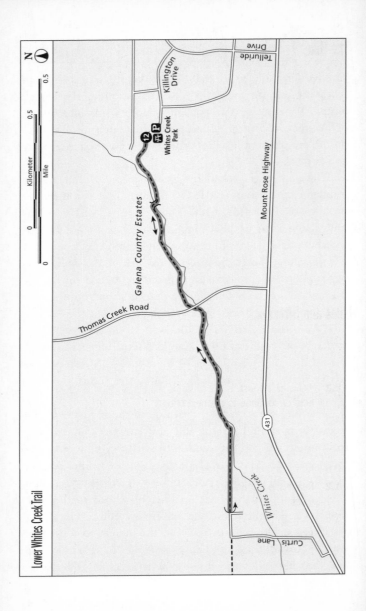

Lower Whites Creek Trail

N

Kilometer
0   0.5
0   0.5
Mile

Telluride Drive

Killington Drive

12
Whites Creek Park
P

Galena Country Estates

Thomas Creek Road

Mount Rose Highway

431

Whites Creek

Curtis Lane

escaping the suburban surroundings when the trail crosses four-lane Thomas Creek Road (no crosswalk, so be careful), but you're tucked quickly back into the riparian zone on the other side.

Gentler climbing through willow and scrub, with short side trails leading creekside, leads to a fenced area where waterside access is denied. A final climb takes you up and out of the drainage onto a dirt road at the entrance to private property: A sign declares IF YOU CAN READ THIS YOU'RE IN RANGE. This is the turnaround point—but not for that reason! Stopping here keeps this much longer trail—it continues toward Mount Rose and links with the popular Jones-Whites Creek Loop—within the "easy" category.

Unless you chose to continue, retrace your steps to the trailhead.

Miles and Directions

0.0 Start behind the large pine, following the trail best traveled into the creek canyon. Stay left (west) where a side trail breaks right (north) to diversion channels.

0.2 Arrive at the first bridge crossing on the right (north). Cross here or continue to the next bridge.

0.3 Reach the second bridge spanning the creek, this one made of less substantial boards. If you haven't already crossed, this is your last chance.

0.8 Cross Thomas Creek Road and continue on the signed trail.

1.2 Reach the boundary of a fence that blocks access to the creek.

1.4 Arrive at the turnaround point on an unpaved neighborhood road.

2.8 Retrace your steps to the trailhead.

13 Galena Creek Nature Trail

The lower reaches of Mount Rose offer long, arduous trail access to the tantalizing altitudes surrounding Lake Tahoe. Sample a nugget of that alpine experience on this gentle romp through the woods surrounding lower Galena Creek.

Distance: 0.9-mile loop
Approximate hiking time: 45 minutes to 1 hour
Difficulty: Easy
Trail surface: Dirt singletrack
Best seasons: Late spring, summer, and fall
Other trail users: None
Canine compatibility: Leashed dogs permitted
Land status: Galena Creek Regional Park
Fees and permits: None
Schedule: The park is open from 8:00 a.m. to 9:00 p.m. June to Sept; 8:00 a.m. to 7:00 p.m. Sept to Nov; 8:00 a.m. to 5:00 p.m. Nov to Mar; and 8:00 a.m. to 7:00 p.m. Mar to June
Trailhead amenities: Facilities include ample parking spaces, restrooms, water, picnic tables, a dog waste station, and trash cans. The ranger station, fish hatchery building, and Camp We

Ch Me are nearby.
Maps: USGS Washoe City; no map is necessary, as the trail is well marked with interpretive posts.
Trail contacts: Washoe County Department of Regional Parks and Open Space, 2601 Plumas St., Reno 89509; (775) 823-6500; www.washoecountyparks .com. The park's direct number is (775) 849-2511.
Special considerations: The Galena Creek Nature Trail was in the process of being upgraded when it was researched for this guide. The exact route may be different than what's described here. An interpretive guide to the nature trail will be available once trail construction is complete.
Other: With shaded picnic grounds, access to the Mount Rose Wilderness, an overnight camping lodge, a visitor center,

outdoor campfire programs, winter sports activities, and a fishing pond, Galena Creek Regional Park is a wonderful place to spend a day.

Finding the trailhead: From US 395 southbound, take the NV 431 (Mount Rose Highway) exit. Head west on the Mount Rose Highway for 7.2 miles to the south entrance to Galena Creek Regional Park (the second park entrance). Go past the garage and park sign, then down into the lower parking lot. The trailhead is at the west end of the parking lot. The main park address is 18350 Mount Rose Highway in Reno. GPS: N39 21.245' / W119 51.458'

The Hike

Galena Creek begins, as most mountain streams do, as a trickle in the snow-soaked heights of the Mount Rose Wilderness. But by the time it reaches the lowland park bearing its name, it's become the rumbling, tumbling heart of this extremely kid-friendly (and popular) nature trail.

The creek is particularly raucous in spring and early summer, when gorged with meltwater. But regardless the season and the vigor of the flow, Galena Creek supports a riparian strip lively with aspen and willow surrounded by a lovely lower montane forest dominated by Jeffrey and ponderosa pines. Check the cones to identify which tree is which: ponderosa pine cones have sharp points (prickly ponderosas), the Jeffrey cones don't (gentle Jeffreys).

As of summer 2009, Washoe County was redesigning the nature trail into stacked loops, one about 0.5 mile in length—easy for younger schoolchildren to negotiate—and the second about 1 mile in length and incorporating steeper sections. The route described here is essentially the longer route. Signposts will be moved and the interpretive guide reissued once construction is complete; it will be available at the information kiosk near the bridge.

Begin your exploration by crossing Galena Creek on a sturdy wooden bridge. On the far side a trail sign directs you left (west). Pass the junction of the Bitterbrush Trail, then the path narrows to singletrack and gently climbs to the intersection of the two legs of the loop. Stay straight (west), traveling the trail in a clockwise direction, with the creek on the left (south) and the forest on the right (north).

The path climbs gently to an indistinct junction with an unmaintained trail leading west into a canyon. Pause here to ponder the purpose of a circular concrete structure on the far side of the creek (a flood containment pond? a livestock watering hole? a bear bathtub?). The nature trail bears right (north) up a short flight of steps, earning views of the Truckee Meadows as it climbs.

Once out of the creek drainage, the route meanders through woodlands scattered with boulders (glacial erratics) and low-growing mountain manzanita. Stone and log steps break up the steepest section of a slow descent that skirts a striking split rock. On flat terrain again, the rock-lined trail swings south, back toward the creek. Close the loop back alongside the creek, and unless you want to do laps, retrace your steps to the trailhead.

Miles and Directions

- **0.0** Start by heading right (northeast) down the gravel road at the south end of the lower parking lot. Once across the bridge turn left (west), following Galena Creek upstream.
- **0.1** At the junction of the Bitterbrush Trail, stay left (west) on the signed nature trail. The junction of the two legs of the loop is

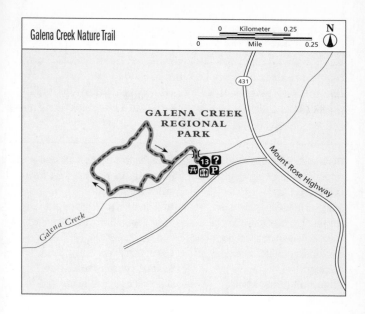

0   Kilometer   0.25

0   Mile   0.25

N

GALENA CREEK
REGIONAL
PARK

431

Mount Rose Highway

Galena Creek

less than a tenth of a mile farther; stay straight (streamside) to complete the route in a clockwise direction.

0.4 At the unsigned junction with the unsigned, unmaintained trail, stay right (north) on the nature trail, climbing a short flight of steps.

0.8 Close the loop where the two legs meet. Turn left (east) and retrace your steps toward the trailhead.

0.9 Arrive at the parking area.

Options: Though too long (more than 10 miles) and too steep (1,800 feet in elevation change) to qualify as an easy hike, the Jones-White Creek Loop Trail—the trailhead is in the north section of the park—is a tempting option for fit, experienced hikers. Those who want to do something easier can take the 0.5-mile loop option.

14 Little Washoe Lake Trail

Skimming the east shore of Little Washoe Lake, beneath the domineering heights of Slide Mountain, this narrow footpath leading into a small nature area is a pleasure for bird-watchers and beach lovers alike.

Distance: 1 mile out and back
Approximate hiking time: 1 hour
Difficulty: Easy
Trail surface: Dirt and sand singletrack; overgrown in places
Best seasons: Year-round; avoid the exposed route at midday in summer
Other trail users: None
Canine compatibility: Leashed dogs permitted
Land status: Washoe Lake State Park
Fees and permits: A day-use fee is levied; pay at the entrance kiosk
Schedule: Sunrise to sunset
Trailhead amenities: Restrooms, picnic facilities, and information

are available at the trailhead.
Maps: USGS Washoe City; www .nvtrailmaps.com
Trail contacts: Washoe Lake State Park, 4855 East Lake Blvd., Carson City 89704; (775) 687-4319; http://parks.nv.gov/wl.htm
Special considerations: No shade is available along the route, so avoid the heat of the day. Intersecting paths and a lack of trail signs can make route finding confusing, but stay close to the shoreline and you won't get lost.
Other: Bring binoculars and a birding guide—the lake and surrounding wetlands harbor a host of feathered friends.

Finding the trailhead: The Little Washoe Lake trailhead is in the northernmost part of the state park, which occupies much of the Washoe Valley between Reno and Carson City. From US 395 southbound from Reno, take the first East Lake Boulevard exit (at the signed Washoe Hill Summit); from Carson City heading northbound, this is the second East Lake Boulevard exit. Head south on East Lake

Boulevard for 0.2 mile to the Little Washoe Lake park entrance on the right (west). Follow the park road for 0.1 mile, past the fee station, to the parking area. The trailhead, marked with a little, easily missed trail sign, is at the southern end of the lot near a picnic table. GPS: N39 19.574' / W119 47.540'

The Hike

Venture onto the Little Washoe Lake Trail in the morning or the evening, when the light is soft and the lake surface glitters. Slide Mountain and Mount Rose form an impressive rampart above the lake's far shore. The birds are active: songbirds flitting from bush to bush, water birds flying low over the lake, shorebirds wading in the shallows. The setting is picture-perfect.

The trail weaves through the scrub above the lakeshore beach, a lure for sunbathers, kids, and swimming dogs, to the Scripps Wildlife Management Area. The route stays on the high ground, which rings with birdsong and, when it's wet, the croaking of frogs and toads.

Route finding can be challenging at the outset, since paths and overgrown dirt tracks intersect in the scrub and there are few trail markers. But you can't get lost: This is open country, and it's easy to see where you're going and where you've come from. Begin by hiking down a narrow path; the trail widens within 100 yards and views open across the lake. Where paths cross, stay right (southbound and parallel to the shoreline), picking through the brush where the trail becomes indistinct. If you venture left (eastward), you'll end up paralleling, then intersecting, the dirt road into the Scripps Wildlife Management Area—your ultimate destination. Use the tall pole hung with orange and white flags rising above the scrub as a target if you wander.

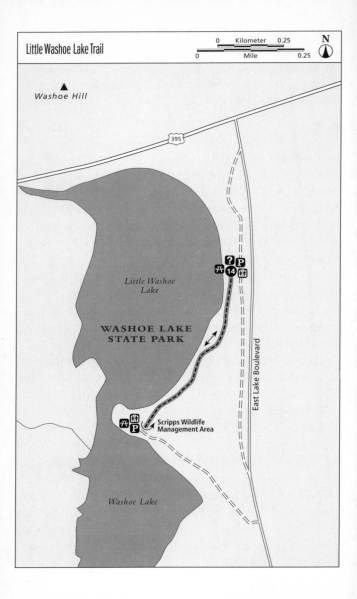

Little Washoe Lake Trail

0 Kilometer 0.25
0 Mile 0.25

N

Washoe Hill

395

Little Washoe
Lake

WASHOE LAKE
STATE PARK

14

East Lake Boulevard

Scripps Wildlife
Management Area

Washoe Lake

Beyond the pole follow the narrow singletrack across a patch of white hardpan and through marsh grasses that resonate with birdsong and the hum of crickets. The track ends on the Scripps road about 200 yards from the restrooms. Cross the road and take a short trail down to the north shore of Washoe Lake to check out boaters and birds on the big water. When ready, return as you came.

Vehicle noise is a constant here: Nearby US 395 is always busy and East Lake Boulevard, skirting the east side of the lake, can be busy as well. But don't let that dissuade you—the views and the birds make up for it.

Miles and Directions

0.0   Start behind the picnic table at the south end of the parking lot.

0.2   At the unmarked junction with a social trail stay right (southwest/toward the shoreline).

0.3   Follow the path parallel to the beach to a worn trail sign at a tall pole hung with orange and white flags.

0.5   The trail ends on the Scripps Wildlife Management Area road. Cross the road to check out bigger Washoe Lake, then return as you came.

0.9   Trail signs direct you to the right (beachside), then left (toward East Lake Boulevard) to put you on the right trail back to the picnic area.

1.0   Arrive back at the trailhead.

15 Davis Creek Nature Trail

Perfect for a family outing, this pretty little nature trail offers a quick and easy tour through the ecological transition zone between the lower montane ecosystem and the high desert, where the yellow pine forests of the Sierra's lower slopes give way to the sages and scrubs of the Great Basin.

Distance: 1-mile loop
Approximate hiking time: 45 minutes to 1 hour
Difficulty: Easy
Trail surface: Dirt singletrack
Best seasons: Year-round, though snow may linger on the trail during winter cold snaps
Other trail users: None
Canine compatibility: Leashed dogs permitted
Land status: Davis Creek Regional Park
Fees and permits: None
Schedule: Sunrise to sunset

Trailhead amenities: Restrooms, picnic areas, trash cans, and camping facilities are available throughout the park.
Maps: USGS Washoe City; an interpretive trail map is available at the trailhead.
Trail contacts: Washoe County Department of Regional Parks and Open Space, 2601 Plumas St., Reno 89509; (775) 823-6500; www.washoecountyparks .com. The park's direct line is (775) 849-0684.

Finding the trailhead: From US 395 in the Washoe Valley (between Reno and Carson City) take the NV 429 (Old US 395) exit (signed for Davis Creek and Bowers Mansion). Follow NV 429 west for 0.3 mile to Davis Creek Park Road (also signed for the park) and turn right (west). Follow the park road past the entry station and campground, staying left (south) into the day use area. The parking lot is approximately 0.1 mile from the park gate on the left (east); it's the lot just before the last group picnic area at the Ophir Creek trailhead. The park's address is 25 Davis Creek Park Rd. GPS: N39 18.218' / W119 49.979'

The Hike

The "Davis Creek Naturalist Guide," available at the trail-head, describes the geology and habitats that you'll encounter along this lovely foothill path, which incorporates high desert, lower montane, and riparian environments. Take some time along the first part of the route to enjoy views across the Washoe Valley and at the end to listen to the quiet of the forest.

Begin on a rocky singletrack that weaves through scrub to post 1, where you can look up and west at the impressive and unstable slopes of Slide Mountain. Just beyond you'll reach the junction with the Discovery Trail; go right (into the trees) on the signed NATURE TRAIL. Interpretive stops are marked with wooden posts topped with tree-shaped icons and yellow numbers; other trail markers include yellow pinecone signposts and arrows. Bear left (east) where the first arrow indicates.

By post 3 you've stepped out of the woods and into the sage and scrub of the high desert, enjoying views across the Washoe Valley, part of the vast landscape of broad dry valleys separated by ragged mountain ranges that makes up the Great Basin.

Climb away from the views, then drop to skirt the shore of the park's little pond, where children wade in the shallows and anglers hope for a bite. A large fenced home is to the left (east) as the path enters the woods; the trail can be indistinct along this stretch amid granite boulders and thick pine needle litter. From post 5 it arcs south, past the house and through a flat, to post 6 at the impressive stump of an ancient Jeffrey pine. Continue south, past a pinecone trail sign then over a bridge to a junction with the Ophir Creek Trail.

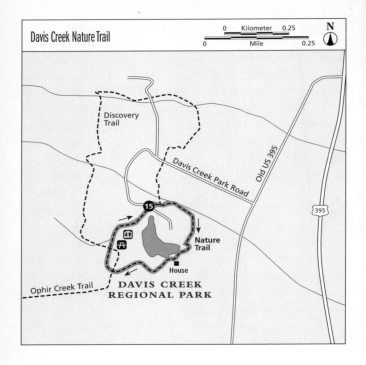

0   Kilometer   0.25

0   Mile   0.25

N

Discovery
Trail

Davis Creek Park Road

Old US 395

395

15

Nature
Trail

House

Ophir Creek Trail

DAVIS CREEK
REGIONAL PARK

A NATURE TRAIL sign points right (north); the path follows the grassy stream, crosses a wooden staircase that is
part of the Discovery Trail, then drops down around the
picnic grounds. Cross the park road and enter the riparian
zone surrounding the pond's inlet stream. Interpretive stop
9 focuses on the willows that crowd the marshy area. The
rock-lined decomposed granite path leads to a little wooden
bridge and a trail intersection; go left (north) over another
bridge, past post 10, and back to the trailhead.

Miles and Directions

0.0 Start at the NATURE TRAIL sign; be sure to pick up a guide. In about 150 feet stay right (into the trees) on the signed NATURE TRAIL.

0.2 Pass posts 2 and 3 as you traverse a scrub slope with views of Washoe Valley.

0.3 The trail tops a rise and drops to the shore of the pond. Signs direct hikers left on the pondside path.

0.4 From interpretive post 5 head south (away from the pond and past the house) to post 6 at the stump, then continue south toward Ophir Creek.

0.6 Cross the creek and reach the Ophir Creek Trail junction. Go right (north), following the NATURE TRAIL sign and arrow. Pass post 7 and cross the Discovery Trail.

0.8 Drop through the picnic grounds and cross the park road to the PINECONE TRAIL sign and path leading into the willows.

0.9 Go left (north) at the trail junction.

1.0 Arrive back at the trailhead.

Options: The Ophir Creek Trail begins (or ends) in Davis Creek Regional Park. Leading from the woodlands at the base of the Carson Range into the alpine heights on the slopes of Mount Rose, the Ophir Creek route is too long and steep to qualify as an easy hike, but for the ambitious, experienced hiker this classic route is a must-do.

16 Deadman's Overlook Trail

There ain't a dead man in heaven or hell who wouldn't be pleased by the views at the apex of this loop. From a quaint gazebo atop a scruffy hillside, you'll be treated to vistas of Washoe Lake, the Washoe Valley, and Slide Mountain.

Distance: 1.2-mile lollipop loop
Approximate hiking time: 1 hour
Difficulty: Moderate due to steep inclines
Trail surface: Dirt singletrack
Best seasons: Spring and fall
Other trail users: None
Canine compatibility: Leashed dogs permitted
Land status: Washoe Lake State Park
Fees and permits: A day-use fee is levied; pay at the park entrance station about 0.3 mile north of the trailhead.
Schedule: Sunrise to sunset
Trailhead amenities: You'll find parking for four or five cars and a trail map at the trailhead.

More parking is available along the shoulder of East Lake Road. Restrooms, information, and the fee station are located at the main park entrance. The park also has camping facilities.
Maps: USGS Carson City; a trail map is posted on an information board at the trailhead; www .nvtrailmaps.com.
Trail contacts: Washoe Lake State Park, 4855 East Lake Blvd., Carson City 89704; (775) 687-4319; www.parks.nv.gov/ wl.htm
Special considerations: A complete dearth of shade makes this route a scorcher in the heat of a summer day.

Finding the trailhead: Washoe Lake State Park is located in the scenic Washoe Valley between Reno and Carson City. From US 395 southbound from Reno take the second East Lake Boulevard exit; from Carson City northbound take the first East Lake Boulevard exit. Follow East Lake Boulevard north for 2.8 miles to the trailhead parking area on the right (east) side of the road. GPS: N39 14.161' / W119 45.481'

The Hike

From the gazebo at the top of the Deadman's Overlook Trail, you'll look out across the broad basin cradling Washoe Lake and Little Washoe Lake onto the steep, scarred east face of Slide Mountain. Washed white with snow in winter and spring, streaked gray and dark green during the long dry summer, this distinctive peak dominates nearly every vista along this segment of the mountain front.

The peak's name is derived from its unstable geology. Reaching a height of more than 9,600 feet, the scars on its south- and east-facing slopes have been caused by repeated landslides. The most recent was catastrophic: In May 1983 the southeast face, made more unstable by heavy rains, gave way and cascaded down the Ophir Creek drainage into the Washoe Valley, taking out two small reservoirs and damaging or destroying everything in its path.

A partially interpreted loop leads to the wooden gazebo, which is perched atop a high point on the east side of Washoe Lake and is visible from the trailhead. The route begins along a riparian corridor fed by a seasonal stream, passing a memorial cross dedicated to "Grandma" and the first of several metal interpretive markers. These signs identify the desert and riparian plants along the trail, including watercress, monkeyflower, Mormon tea, desert peach (sporting delicate pink blooms in spring), bitterbrush, stinging nettle (watch this one!), and the ubiquitous sagebrush.

After a brief walk along the riparian zone, ignoring side trails leading into the brush, you'll reach an obvious but unmarked trail junction. Cross the streambed and begin a moderate climb across the scrub-covered slope, with timber stair steps assisting in the ascent. Several switchbacks allow you to enjoy views of Slide Mountain and Washoe Lake as you hike.

Pass another trail intersection on the left (east); stay right (west), cross a dry drainage, then climb along a rocky traverse to the gazebo. Jumbles of red rock surround the wooden structure; wildflowers sprinkle the landscape with patches of purple, white, and yellow in season.

You can return the way you came, but to complete the loop, stay on the obvious trail (the middle route) that traverses the hillside as it drops into the drainage. The trail is crisscrossed with social paths, but the main track is well used and obvious. The long traverse is peppered with small gardens in spring—pillows of white blossoms filling crevices in the rocky hillside. Pass another interpretive sign (for serviceberry) as you descend.

In the drainage, turn left (west) and follow the path back down toward the trailhead. Slide Mountain and its accompanying lower peaks lie ahead; you'll pass additional interpretive signs as well. Close the loop on the way down, then retrace your steps back to the trailhead.

Miles and Directions

0.0   Start on the signed interpretive trail.

0.2   At the trail junction go right (south) on the path with the timber steps that leads up toward the overlook.

0.4   Pass a trail that breaks off to the left (east).

0.5   Arrive at the gazebo. Enjoy the views, then stay straight on the obvious trail leading northeast into the creek drainage, ignoring the road to the right (south) and several side trails that intersect the descending traverse.

0.8   At the trail junction in the drainage, turn left (west), back toward Slide Mountain and the trailhead.

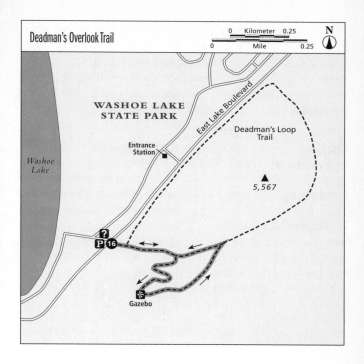

0   Kilometer   0.25

0   Mile   0.25

N

WASHOE LAKE
STATE PARK

East Lake Boulevard

Deadman's Loop
Trail

Entrance
Station

Washoe
Lake

▲
5,567

?
P 16

Gazebo

0.9 Reach the trail junction at the beginning of the loop. Stay straight (west) toward the lake and mountains.

1.2 Arrive back at the trailhead and parking area.

Options: Washoe Lake State Park offers a variety of trail options, the most obvious being an extension of this route known as Deadman's Loop.

17 Pasture River–Mexican Ditch Loop

From the pastures of a working ranch to a historic diversion dam on the Carson River, this route offers a meditative walk on the east side of the Carson Valley.

Distance: 3.6-mile lollipop loop
Approximate hiking time: 2.5 to 3 hours
Difficulty: More challenging due to trail length
Trail surface: Mostly dirt ranch road; some dirt singletrack
Best seasons: Winter, spring, and late fall. You'll find shade along the river and the ditch, but the hike may be uncomfortably hot in summer at midday.
Other trail users: Mountain bikers, equestrians, trail runners, birders
Canine compatibility: Leashed dogs permitted
Land status: Silver Saddle Ranch was a Bureau of Land Management property when this guide was researched, but ownership was slated to change to Carson City in the future.
Fees and permits: None
Schedule: Silver Saddle Ranch is open from 7:00 a.m. to 5:00 p.m. daily.

Trailhead amenities: You'll find parking, restrooms, and information at the trailhead. A handicapped-accessible restroom is located farther along the park's loop road.
Maps: USGS New Empire; trail maps are in the red mailbox at the trailhead
Trail contacts: Bureau of Land Management Carson City District Office, 5665 Morgan Mill Rd., Carson City 89701; (775) 885-6000; www.blm.gov. Carson City Parks and Recreation Department, 201 N. Carson St., Carson City 89701; (775) 887-2262; www.carson-city.nv.us
Special considerations: Several signs warn of frequent rattlesnake sightings. If you don't bother them, they're not likely to bother you. Keep your pet on a leash. Do not swim in the ditch; the water moves deceptively fast. So does the Carson River when swollen with runoff in spring.

Other: This is a working ranch, so be sure to close gates behind you or leave them open as instructed by signs or the ranch manager.

Finding the trailhead: From US 395 in Carson City, take the Fallon/Dayton exit. Go left (east) on US 50 toward Fallon for 1 mile to Fairview Drive. Go right (south) on Fairview Drive for 1.3 mile to the roundabout. Go three-quarters of the way around, then bear right again on East Fifth Street. Follow East Fifth Street for 0.2 mile to Carson River Road (NV 513). Turn right (south) on Carson River Road and drive 1.3 miles to the signed park entrance on the right (south). Follow the park road (which becomes one way) around to the ranch complex and trailhead. GPS: N39 08.320' / W119 42.699'

The Hike

You'll pass through fenced hayfields as you begin this pleasant ramble through Silver Saddle Ranch and along the Carson River. If the fields have been irrigated, they grow lush and green. If they haven't, native sages, bitterbrush, and desert peach reclaim the fallow space.

Transforming high desert into cultivated farmland seems simple enough here: Open a gate on the Mexican Ditch and let it flow. But water in the West is complicated: treasured, measured, and fought over. The water that flows out of the river into the ditch, and then from the ditch into the surrounding fields, is split and divided between private and public lands in the agricultural bottomlands of the Eagle Valley, with gates open, closed, and gauged as carefully now as they were a century ago.

The Mexican Dam and Ditch were built in the early 1860s to supply water to power the ore-crushing wheels of the Mexican Mill, part of a complex of mills processing the output of Nevada's fabled Comstock Lode. Even before the lode played out, water from the ditch was being diverted to agriculture, according to the Friends of Silver Saddle Ranch, and miners and ranchers battled it out in court for rights to the precious resource. The demise of the Comstock ultimately decided the winner of that battle, with agriculture and development now taking their shares.

These days the ditch carries water to valley ranchers even when the hot summer whittles down the flow in the adjacent Carson River. It supports a riparian strip that rings with birdcall, and the birds in turn attract bird-watchers. The wide, easy ditch road also attracts mountain bikers, trail runners, and day hikers.

The route begins amid the red-painted ranch buildings; if you are lucky, the friendly ranch manager will be on hand to give you advice about the route. Interpretive signs around the ranch give information about the Mexican Ditch and the ranch property.

The Pasture River Trail skirts the north side of one of the fenced hayfields, a wide path that cuts a straight shot to the Carson River. At riverside you'll find a small picnic area shaded by cottonwood and possibly picnickers and anglers. Head south along the trail between the river and the pastures, passing through a couple of gates as you follow the ranch road. An avenue of cottonwoods provides shade as you proceed.

After 1 mile pass a gate and an interpretive sign that describes the "ribbon of green" that is the Carson River in all seasons, whether full and swift with winter runoff or dried to fish-clumped puddles in fall. Drop to riverside, staying left on the sandy road through the bottomland (this can be wet in spring), then climb to the junction with the

Mexican Ditch Trail. An interpretive sign here quotes Mark Twain: "Whiskey is for drinking, water is for fighting."

Heading south on the easy, flat, dirt road wedged between the river and the ditch you'll have plenty of opportunity to watch quail scurry from bush to bush, lizards scamper from rock to rock, and songbirds flit from branch to branch in the cottonwoods and willows. Anglers scatter along the far shore, but unless the birders are out, you may have the trail to yourself.

You can hear the muffled thunder of water spilling over the diversion dam at trail's end before you reach it. In spring the dam is a long 10-foot-high whitewater fall, but that diminishes as the summer progresses. The Carson pools behind, spread between shallow slopes covered in desert scrub. The gate that funnels water into the ditch is on the right (west); when the Carson begins to dry, sandbags are used to divert the flow into the ditch.

The dam is the turnaround point; retrace your steps to the junction of the Mexican Ditch Trail and the Pasture River Trail. To complete the loop portion of the hike, stay left (northwest) on the ditch trail, following the green strip along the pastures back to the ranch complex and trailhead. You'll enjoy views of the Carson Range and Slide Mountain as you return.

Miles and Directions

0.0 Start by walking through the ranch property to the fence line of the first hayfield. Go left (north) along the fence to the signed Pasture River Trail, then head east toward the river.

0.4 Reach the gate on the bank of the Carson River and turn right (south) on the wide track.

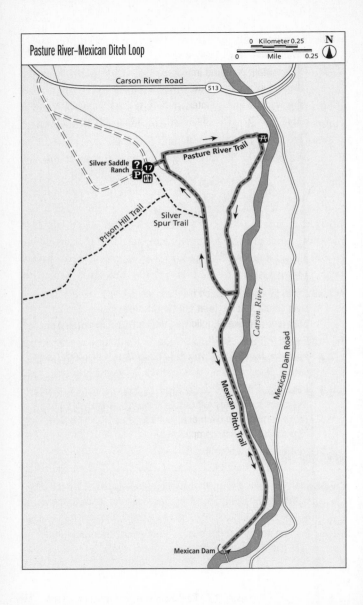

Pasture River-Mexican Ditch Loop

Carson River Road
513

Silver Saddle Ranch

Pasture River Trail

Prison Hill Trail

Silver Spur Trail

Carson River

Mexican Ditch Trail

Mexican Dam Road

Mexican Dam

0   Kilometer 0.25
0   Mile   0.25

N

0.6 The trail narrows and passes through a gate. Remain on the obvious path along the fence line.

0.7 Pass another gate and into a second pasture. Stay left (riverside) on the ranch road, ignoring side roads.

1.0 Reach a gate and an interpretive sign. Pass through the gate (if open) or the style (if closed) and follow the sandy road that drops left (riverside) then climbs to the junction with the Mexican Ditch Trail.

1.2 Go left (south) on the broad dirt Mexican Ditch Trail. The river is on the left (east) and the ditch is on the right (west).

2.0 The trail swings around a curve in the river and ends at the Mexican Dam. Turn around and retrace your steps to the last trail junction.

2.8 Back at the junction of the Mexican Ditch Trail and the Pasture River Trail stay left (north/on the high road) on the Mexican Ditch Trail.

3.0 Carefully cross the ditch overflow and continue on the dirt road to the gate/style at the Carson River interpretive sign. Stay left (northwest), following the pasture's fence as it curves along the ditch.

3.3 Pass the gate and bridge of the Silver Spur Trail on the left (west). Stay right (northwest) on the Mexican Ditch Trail.

3.4 Pass a gate into another hayfield; at the intersection of the ranch roads stay left (straight/north) on the ditch trail. Cross an irrigation ditch and go through another gate as you approach the ranch complex.

3.6 Arrive back at the trailhead.

Options: Nearby Prison Hill Recreation Area also offers hiking trails. Access to the Prison Hill trail system from Silver Saddle Ranch is via the Silver Spur and Prison Hill Trails.

18 Fay-Luther Interpretive Loop

Stretched along the lower slopes of Jobs Peak in the Carson River valley, this superlative singletrack meanders from highland desert scrub into shady montane forest and back again.

Distance: 2.8-mile lollipop loop
Approximate hiking time: 2 hours
Difficulty: More difficult due to steep inclines and trail length
Trail surface: Sand, decomposed granite, and dirt singletrack
Best seasons: Spring and fall; avoid heat of the day in summer
Other trail users: Mountain bikers, equestrians
Canine compatibility: Dogs permitted year-round, but must be leashed from October 15 to Mar 30 to protect mule deer habitat. Also, please pick up after your pet.
Land status: Bureau of Land Management (BLM); the trailhead and a short trail section are on forest service land
Fees and permits: None
Schedule: Sunrise to sunset

Trailhead amenities: You'll find parking for both cars and horse trailers at the trailhead, along with an information sign. A trail map and dog waste disposal station are about 50 yards beyond the gate on the Sandy/Jobs Peak Ranch Trails. No restroom is available. Equestrians are asked to clean up after their stock at the trailhead.
Maps: USGS Woodfords; an excellent trail map is posted 50 yards from the trailhead and is available online via links at the BLM and Carson Valley Trails Association Web sites.
Trail contacts: Bureau of Land Management, Carson City District/Sierra Front Field Office, 5665 Morgan Mill Rd., Carson City 89701; (775) 885-6000; www.blm.gov/nv

Finding the trailhead: From US 395 south of Carson City, go right (southwest) on NV 88. Follow NV 88 for 2.1 miles to NV 207 (Waterloo Lane). Turn right (west) on NV 207 and go 3.2 miles to Foothill Road (NV 206). Go left (south) on Foothill Road for 4.4 miles to the signed trailhead parking area on the right (west). GPS: N38 52.216' / W119 48.637'

The Hike

Dominating the mountain front south of Carson City, the gray granite massif of Jobs Peak serves as backdrop for this wonderful trek through high desert and low forest. Views from the trail are amazing, stretching east across patchwork ranchland to the brown slopes of the Pine Nut Mountains and climbing west into the foothills of the Sierra Nevada.

The Fay-Luther trail system, more than 8 miles of interlocking paths surrounding Luther Creek and rugged Fay Canyon, is a justifiable source of pride for its developers, which include the BLM, the Humboldt-Toiyabe National Forest, the American Land Conservancy, and the Carson Valley Trails Association. The interpretive loop described here is just one of several options showcasing the relatively untouched natural beauty of the area.

The route begins among big sage, bitterbrush, and desert peach, with great views in all directions. The Sandy Trail is aptly named, but the incline is gentle, so the hiking is easy, if exposed and potentially hot. Pass the doggie waste station, the California National Historic Trail marker (part of the route used by emigrants to California's fabled gold country), and the California/Nevada state border as you climb, staying left (southwest) at junctions with the Jobs Peak Ranch Trail.

A bench in the shade of a massive Jeffrey pine, on the verge of the transition from high desert to montane environments, sports incredible views across the Carson River valley and up the mountain front. The views accompany you as the trail traverses the pine-shaded, scrub-scented slope to the junction with the Interpretive Loop; stay left (south) to complete a clockwise circuit. The setting is especially lovely in spring, when the desert blooms yellow and pink, the pastures in the valley are verdant, and the Pine Nut Mountains are painted moist shades of green and brown.

Roll along the ecotone, past the first junction with the Bitter Cherry Trail, to Luther Creek. The willow-lined stream accompanies the trail up and west toward the mouth of Fay Canyon: Say goodbye to valley views and hello to the steep, gray and evergreen slopes of the mountains.

The path begins to climb more earnestly as it passes the second Bitter Cherry Trail junction and curves away from the creek. A switchback and traverse lead up a steep slope, then past the intersection with the Grand View Loop. Now on the ridge back, heading north on the return leg of the loop, vistas resume across the valley and up the steely mountain front freckled with evergreens.

The descent includes switchbacking traverses of forested gullies and several opportunities to contemplate the layered greens and browns of the valley on perfectly placed dedicated benches. Pass two junctions with the Jeffrey Pine Trail before a final drop to close the Interpretive Loop. Retrace your route through the transition zone and the high desert to the trailhead.

Miles and Directions

0.0 Start up the Sandy Trail behind the INFORMATION sign.

0.1 Pass junctions with the California National Historic Trail and the Jobs Peak Ranch Trail, then the California/Nevada state border, staying straight (southwest) on the obvious Sandy Trail.

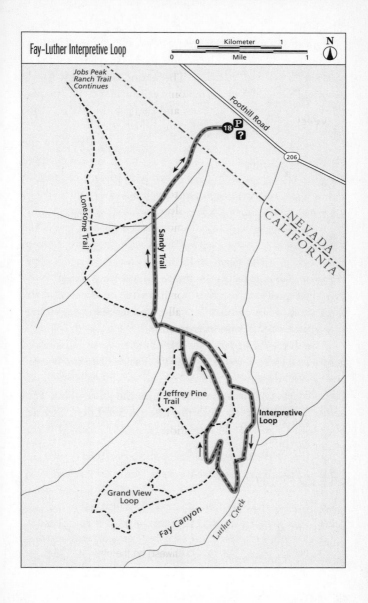

Fay-Luther Interpretive Loop

0   Kilometer   1

0   Mile   1

N

Jobs Peak
Ranch Trail
Continues

Foothill Road

18 P ?

206

NEVADA
CALIFORNIA

Lonesome Trail

Sandy Trail

Jeffrey Pine
Trail

Interpretive
Loop

Grand View
Loop

Fay Canyon

Luther Creek

0.3 At the second junction with the Jobs Peak Ranch Trail stay left (southwest) on the Sandy Trail.

0.5 Pass the Red Barn Ranch bench in the shade of a giant Jeffrey pine.

0.6 Reach the Lonesome Trail junction; stay left (southwest) on the Sandy Trail.

0.7 The Sandy Trail ends at the beginning of the Interpretive Loop. Go left (southeast) to complete the route in a clockwise direction.

0.9 At the intersection with the Bitter Cherry Trail stay left (southeast). The trail comes parallel with Luther Creek.

1.1 At the unsigned junction with a social trail stay right (south) on the Interpretive Trail.

1.2 Reach the second Bitter Cherry Trail junction and stay left (south) on the Interpretive Loop.

1.3 Stay right (up) and north around the switchback at the unsigned junction.

1.4 Arrive at the signed Grand View Loop intersection. Stay right (north) on the Interpretive Loop, passing the Charles Phillips bench and heading down the ridge back.

1.6 Switchback in and out of a gully to the first junction with the Jeffrey Pine Trail. Stay right (northeast) on the Interpretive Loop.

2.0 Switchback through a steeper gully to the second Jeffrey Pine Trail intersection. Again, stay right (northeast) on the Interpretive Loop.

2.1 Drop to the junction to close the Interpretive Loop.

2.8 Retrace your steps down the Sandy Trail to the trailhead.

Options: You can extend your tour of the Fay-Luther area by venturing out on either the Jeffrey Pine Trail or (more strenuous) the Grand View Loop. The trail also links to the Jobs Peak Ranch route and trailhead to the north.